TEXAS: 1874

TEXAS

1874

An eyewitness account
of conditions in
post-reconstruction Texas

By EDWARD KING

Profusely illustrated from original sketches

By J. WELLS CHAMPNEY

Edited by Robert S. Gray
Introduction by Joe B. Frantz

CORDOVAN PRESS
HOUSTON

Printed in the United States of America by Cordovan
Printing, Houston.

Library of Congress Catalog Card No. 74-80449.

iv

Contents

A Century Ago

FIRST, a little simple mathematics. In 1874 any elder of seventy years or less would have been younger than thirty when the Republic of Texas wrested its freedom from Mexico. Or to enlist another generation, any youth old enough to remember the Texas revolution, say seven to ten, would still be on the springtime side of fifty. In modern terms, the memory of the Depression which so many of us still carry today would be almost exactly equivalent to the memory of an 1874 Texan toward the birth pangs of Anglo-American Texas.

With those relationships in mind, the feeling of almost unbridled optimism which saturates this book becomes understandable. The Republic of Texas had been raw; post-bellum Texas still had its rough edges, but how far it had traveled in less than four decades! Instead of a comparative handful of new citizens clustered principally in the southern and eastern portions of the state, now more than a million people had fanned out over its broad lands, beyond the trees to the plains, beyond the farms to the ranches, and beyond the coast to the beginnings of the Staked Plains. In 1834 there had been San Augustine and San Felipe and Bastrop and Bexar and Laredo and Quintana. By 1874 there were Galveston and Houston, Austin, Dallas and Denison, Jefferson and Marshall, and New Braunfels, some of them downright civilized towns and others displaying intimations of becoming bearable.

So the speculators had been right, the seers had been right, the idealists had been right. Come to Texas and hold on, they had adjured; the people will fill the land, and wealth and something called culture will be sure to follow. Take Galveston, the best town in the state. It had all the accouterments of a going town — mansions and magnolias, schools and shipping, theaters and hotels, and chefs who knew what to do with oysters beyond frying them in corn meal and drowning them in ketchup. From Galveston, cattle were shipped to Havana. To Galveston, coffee came from Central America. Galveston's town fathers dreamed about a canal that would run from the Mississippi to the Rio Grande, and along the way would irrigate all the Texas farmland so that lush crops of corn and cotton and rice would grow, all of which would have to be loaded from Galveston's myriad of wharves and piers en route to a paying world.

Meanwhile in Houston the canal dream was a bit more modest. Houston would settle for only fifty miles of dredging, so that it too could be a seaport. But Galveston only scoffed. Given a choice between shipping from that mud-sink Houston and the ineffable Treasure Isle, who would choose Houston? Galveston was unassailable. Besides, whatever traffic the proposed Houston ship canal would draw off would be more than replaced by Galveston's railroad connection with the mainland.

Less than a decade before, a northern neighbor had felt as complacent as Galveston. Saint Louis, already an historic hub of the nation's heartland, had turned down the opportunity to build cattle towns in Kansas and make itself the world's butcher. Chicago, less content, had seized the opportunity, so that later Carl Sandburg would write his poems about the city at the foot of Lake Michigan, not the river city just below the confluence of the Father of Waters and the Mighty Missouri. Non-decisions such as Galveston's and Saint Louis's are among the reasons that town fathers sometimes welcome the grave.

But the author doesn't worry about mistakes or rivalries in Texas. He views the entire state through rose-tinted lenses, and he knows that Texas can contain as many people as its area counterpart, the Republic of France. Fifty million people, sixty million, limitless. The total makes no difference, for Texas has the room and the

resources. So he may be critical of some of the monotonous terrain of Texas, and dub the San Jacinto battlefield
a "dreary expanse," but on those equally featureless
prairies of north Texas, he can see thousands of acres of
wheat and cotton waving their agricultural dollars in the
eternal breeze. And when he looks west of the Texas tree
line, he sees variegated expanses of vivid wildflowers and
infinite grasses put there by God Himself to feed sheep and
cattle into the chutes of cash outside the state.

Naturally he reflects his period and his accepted
whiteness. To him, blacks are objects of curiosity but
undisciplined, shiftless, attractive children who have to be
alternately cudgeled and cuddled like adolescents. He regularly calls them Sambo and Cuffee, but does feel that they
fare better in their "free state, although indulging in all
kinds of queer freaks with [their] money." But the black
is a hindrance to progress; and in some counties, where
whites outnumber blacks by fifty to one, he can observe
happily "that Cuffee stands no whit in the way of John."

As for the Mexican men, they "seem to be perpetually waiting for some one to come and feed them. They
wander about in the most purposeless fashion, . . . yet . . .
are . . . quite inoffensive." Their girls may be "bold-eyed
and beautiful," but generally Mexicans are "hard-headed,
terribly prejudiced; . . . cannot be made to see that [their]
slow, primitive ways, . . . filth and lack of comfort are not
better than the frugal decency and careful home management of the Germans and Americans who surround" them.

Now the Germans! Here is a group to admire,
whether scattered about Houston or clustered in a colony
like New Braunfels. They have all the virtues — a sense of
organization, a love of work, an appreciation of fine food
and drink, and an eternal cheerfulness. They are "rosy."

On the other hand, no Indian is ever mentioned
without an adjective — "ignoble savage," "born with the
genius of murder and rapine firmly implanted in his
breast," "remorseless savage," and "hostile Comanches."
The "most beneficent work" of the extending Texas and
Pacific railroad tracks, he opines, "will be the chasing of
the Indian [no adjective, for once] from the vicinity of the
'cross-timber' country" and making it habitable for small

farmers. Now and then, though, he reverses his field and speaks, for instance, of the "noble Wacos" with the same enthusiasm he shows for Texas' "noble oaks."

Not that the prose is all Pollyanna purple on the white side. He finds the women of south Texas "defiant" in their praise of Texas, while the men around Houston never tire "of declaiming the beauties of the climate" and are "extremely sensitive to criticism." (As one who has an affection for sprawling, eye-stinging, unmanageable Houston, I have been cuffed publicly and privately by its citizens for suggesting that withal it still could stand improvement!) And not to spare north Texas, he decries its "coarse cookery, bad beds, and villainous liquor-drinking."

But taken altogether, he finds Texans a hospitable, gentle, classless, forward-looking people who know they have hold of a good thing and will undoubtedly realize on their state's enormous potential. And if they lag in their efforts, they always have one panacea — the growing reticulation of railroad routes. Just as the Texas and Pacific can lay the Indian threat, so all the railroads can civilize Texans, teach them manners and breeding, connect them with outside sophistications from that broader world, and with whistle, bell, and engine propel them into the desired life of industrialization, enlarging cities, and burgeoning profits. Like a good promoter, he seldom mentions smoke or other pollutions, and dwells not at all on the festerings of slums, uneven classes, and mounting discontents.

For a portrait of Texas one hundred years ago, this delineation is as good as you are likely to get. Although an unborn Chamber of Commerce might have written huge hunks of the manuscript, basically it is fair and mildly objective. What has to be remembered is that only a scant long generation before, Indians were lounging around the mission door in a feral Texas, space was the enemy instead of a diminishing friend, towns are virtually non-existent, and outsiders were unknown. As a Victorian the author saw Texas as new and vibrant, and naturally as exotic and challenging as today's traveler from the South Forty-Eight views his sister, Alaska. Texas was a frontier, only partially reclaimed, with the historic excesses of the frontier. Perforce the people who immigrated to Texas had to make much out of their little, had to magnify their virtues and deny their faults, and just naturally had to hope. For without hope, who would have stayed?

What a sensitive reader can also get from these pages is a glimpse of what might have been, of the resources of land and space that were squandered in pursuit of the false god of progress, of the crimes committed in the name of "development." The ingredients for quality living were once here in abundance. Although we haven't quite washed all those ingredients into the effluvia of oblivion, give us time, Lord, give us time.

Joe B. Frantz
Austin, Texas
St. Valentine's Day 1974

Publisher's Preface, 1974

THIS book, when first published, was part of an ambitious job of fact-gathering and interpretation, commissioned more than a century ago. The project apparently began in 1872 when the publishers of Scribner's Monthly called in two talented young men, Edward King and James Wells Champney, and gave them what they probably considered a "dream" assignment.

Go south, they were told; go all *over* the south, from one end to the other, and report in detail all you see and hear. Take the time you need, travel the miles that need to be covered. Come back and prepare for us a definitive account of what Reconstruction has meant to the Old South.

Scribner's, according to the original Publisher's Preface, "desired to present to the public, through the medium of their popular periodical, an account of the material resources, and the present social and political condition, of the people of the States formerly under the dominion of Slavery."

At that time King was 24 years old and Champney 29. Although young men, both were experienced travelers. Yet an assignment of such magnitude would have been awesome for that period of slow transportation and communication. The fifteen ex-slave states then covered 880,000 square miles and had fourteen million inhabitants. King and Champney set forth, beginning with the more southeasterly states and worked their way west. They traveled more than a year, it appears, "during the whole of the year 1873 and the spring and summer of 1874," said the original preface.

They covered more than 25,000 miles, visited nearly every city and town of importance in the southern states, "talked with men of all classes, parties and colours; carefully investigated the state of the country, the labour question, manufacturing enterprises and site, studied the course of politics in each State since the advent of reconstruction; explored rivers, and penetrated into mountain regions heretofore rarely visited by people of the Northern States, and all but unknown to Europeans.

"They were everywhere kindly and generously received; and they have endeavoured, by pen and pencil to give the reading public a truthful picture of life in the section of the country which has, since the close of the devastating war, been overwhelmed by a variety of misfortunes, but upon which the dawn of a better day is breaking."

Scribner's of the 1870's was one of the country's best known magazines and one of the earliest national periodicals. The series must have attracted world-wide attention. Blackie & Son of Glasgow, Scotland, apparently felt there was an international audience for the material. They acquired the entire series of articles, enlarged upon them and incorporated the whole into a book, published in 1875 under the title "The Southern States of North America."

It is a massive volume of more than 800 pages and certainly one of the finest illustrated books of its age. Champney's busy hands had created hundreds of sketches for the series in Scribner's — titled "The Great South" — and the Scottish publishers apparently called for more of his work to put in their book.

I first saw this great volume as a boy and was delighted to find that it read then, and still reads now, with a clarity and style that is remarkably contemporary. It has always seemed to me that the chapters on Texas, in particular, painted such a starkly realistic portrait of our state in its formative years that you can almost hear the language and smell the smells that both intoxicated and irritated Edward King in Texas.

He and Champney did a thorough, often meticulous job of describing the daily lives, the words, even the accents of those early Texans who had begun rebuilding their state. Champney's sketches froze for posterity the raw and lusty youth of a land on the verge of gigantic expansion. And they knew it.

So this is why the publishers now have edited this volume on Texas out of the original book, and why we have so titled it. We see here how King and Champney saw Texas in 1874 as Reconstruction was ending. And as we began to first research the effort last year, we were pleasantly surprised to learn that the original publishers, Blackie & Son, as a company, is still alive and well and doing business in Glasgow.

In granting us reprint rights, a Blackie & Son spokesman wrote that "We have not done any reprints in this century." The British, it is clear, take the long view of history and Blackie & Son may well consider bringing out another edition in another century. We hope so.

For those interested in books, we should also point out that this is not a fascimile edition. We considered that initially but the small type and even smaller use of the art work in the original edition persuaded us that we should make better use of such excellent material. We have accordingly enlarged many of Champney's sketches to much larger size so their detail can be better seen. At the same time we have tried to keep to the same basic layout and typographical design as in the original. The type you see in this volume is close to that of the original, only larger for easier reading.

We felt that one more feature was important to the reader's understanding and enjoyment of this book. You will see informal footnotes throughout, researched and written by the noted historian Joe B. Frantz, who also wrote our introduction. Dr. Frantz catches Author King in some errors of Texas history and also gives more detail on important historical characters and incidents that may intrigue the Texas reader. In his introduction, Dr. Frantz also properly mentions some areas where King's 19th Century prejudices are showing. To most serious students of Texas history, these instances will not flaw King's reportage but rather add color and the perspective of his times to what he felt about what he saw.

Many who read this book may, in fact, get interested in King and Champney as individuals. The editors certainly did. For that reason, we have researched their subsequent careers and in the Epilogue section of this volume you may learn what they did after their southern assignment was ended.

The publishers in 1974 got a special pleasure from doing this book for a reason which may not be apparent to the reader. Despite their youth, King and Champney were exceptionally good at their respective trades, judged even by today's more demanding standards. Some readers may grow weary of King's occasional long-winded soliloquies, which was often a reporter's way then of showing how learned and sensitive he was. For the most part, though, King wrote with an ear for dialogue, a perception and a bite that today's reporter can well envy. By bringing his and his artist collague to public attention again, we hope their work will be appreciated for both its professional and historical excellence. Whatever Scribner's paid them for the original job, the publishers got their money's worth. King and Champney worked very hard and they turned in a labor of love. It shows, even a century later.

Robert S. Gray, Editor
Houston, Texas
1974

"It is only a few steps from an oleander grove to the surf."

I

"HO FOR TEXAS!" – GALVESTON.

ONE of the saddest sights in New Orleans or Galveston is the daily arrival of hundreds of refugees from the older Southern States, seeking homes on the Texan prairies. The flood of emigration from South Carolina, Alabama and Georgia is formidable, and turned the tide of politics in Texas, in a single year, from Republican flood to Democratic ebb. Old men and little children, youths and maidens, clad in homespun, crowd the railway cars, looking forward eagerly to the land of promise. The ignorance of these poor people with regard to the geography of the country in general, is dense. "I never traveled so much befo'," is a common phrase; "is Texas a mighty long ways off yet?" The old men, if one enters into conversation with them, will regale him with accounts of life in their homes "befo' the surrender." With them, everything dates from the war, leaving the past irrevocably behind its yawning gulf, while in front there is only poverty — or flight.

The route from New Orleans to Brashear City is, in the delightful months of April and May, one of the most beautiful in the South. The railroad which connects at Brashear City with the Morgan steamers sailing to Galveston, and along which the tide of emigration constantly flows, traverses weird forests and lofty cane-brakes, and passes over bayous, swamps, and long stretches of sugar plantations.

Crossing the Mississippi by the great railroad ferry to Algiers, the traveler soon leaves behind the low, green banks, studded with neat, white houses embowered in a profusion of orange groves; and is borne out of sight of the

11

Going to Texas.

black lines of smoke left upon the cloudless sky by the funnels of the river steamers. He passes Bayou des Allemands, and a low country filled with deep, black pools; hurries across the reedy and saturated expanse of Trembling Prairie, dotted with fine oaks; rattles by Raceland, and its moist, black fields, to La Fourche Bayou, on which lies the pretty, cultivated town of Thibodeaux.

He next passes Chacahoula swamp, a wilderness of shriveled cypresses and stagnant water; Tigerville, with its Indian mounds; the rich Boeuf country, along the banks of whose lovely bayou lie wonderful sugar lands, once crowded with prosperous planters, but now showing many an idle plantation. He passes immense groves, from the boughs of whose trees thousands of Spanish moss beards are pendent; and through which long and sombre aisles, like those of a cathedral, open to right and left. He wonders at the presence of the bearded moss on all the trees, and his commercial eye perhaps suggests that it be made available in upholstery; but he is told that the quaint parasite already does good service as the scavenger of the air.

At Brashear City he finds a steamer for Texas at the fine docks built by the enterprising proprietor of the "Morgan line," and notes, as he passes out to the blue waters of the Gulf, the richness of the vegetation along the shores of the inlet. An afternoon and a night — and he is in Galveston.

The coast line of Texas, bordering upon the Gulf of Mexico from Sabine Pass to the Rio Grande, — from the Louisiana boundary to the hybrid, picturesque territory where the American and Mexican civilizations meet and conflict, is richly indented and studded with charming bays. Trinity, Galveston, West, Matagorda, Espiritu Santu, Aransas, and Corpus Christi harbors, each and all offer varied possibilities for future commerce. The whole coast, extending several hundred miles, is also bordered by a series of islands and peninsulas, long and narrow in form, which protect the inner low-lying banks from the high seas.

The plains extending back from the coast in the valleys of the Sabine, the San Jacinto and the Colorado, seem in past centuries to have formed a vast delta, whose summit was probably near the Colorado, and whose angles were formed by the Sabine and the Nueces. Great horizons, apparently boundless as the sea, characterize these plains; the wanderer on the Gulf sees only the illimitable expanse of wave and alluvial; the eye is fatigued by the immensity, and gladly seeks rest upon the lines of ancient forest which cover the borders of the Colorado and the Nucces. Beyond these plains comes the zone of the prairies, whose lightly undulating surface extends inland as far as the Red river, while the mountains on the north-west crown the fertile knolls of rolling country.

These mountains are portions of the Sierra Madre, which is itself but a spur from the grand Andean chain. Running to the north-west in the State of Coahuila (once a portion of Texas), the Sierra Madre spur bifurcates to enter the Texas of the present, and continues in a north-westerly direction, under the name of the San Saba, in whose breasts are locked the rich minerals which the

Spaniard, during his period of domination, so often and so
vainly strove to unearth.

The Texan coast sweeps downward and outward by
a wide curve to the Mexican boundary. Approaching it
from the sea, the eye encounters only a low-lying level of
white sand, with which, however, at all hours, the deep
colors of the gulf are admirably contrasted.

The great sea highway to which I have previously
alluded, from Brashear City, on Berwick's Bay, on the
Louisiana coast, to Galveston, is well known and fascinat-
ing to the modern traveler. The enterprise and liberal
expenditure of a citizen of New York, Mr. Charles Morgan,
has covered the waves of this route with steamships,
which, until recently, furnished the only means of communication between Texas and the rest of the United
States. The Morgan Line was not merely the outgrowth of
an earnest demand; it was the work of an adventurous
pioneer; and although its importance, in view of the grand
railroad development of Northern Texas, can henceforth
be but secondary, its founder will always be remembered
for his foresight and daring. The improvements in the
channels from Berwick's Bay outward are also the work of
the owner of this line. They comprehend the dredging of a
great bar which once obstructed the short passage to the
Gulf, and when completed will be of infinite importance
to the commerce of the whole south-west. Thousands of
tons of shells have been dragged out of the dark-blue water
to make room for the prows of the Morgan fleet, pointed
toward Galveston and Indianola.

And what is Galveston? A thriving city set down
upon a brave little island which has fought its way out of
the depths of the Gulf, and given to the United States her
noblest beach, and to Texas an excellent harbor. Seen
from the sea, when approaching under the fervid light of a
Southern dawn, or when sailing away from it in the white
moonlight, so intensely reflected on the sand, it is indeed a
place where

'Myrtle groves
Shower down their fragrant wealth upon the waves
Whose long, long swell mirrors the dark-green glow
Of cedars and the snow of jasmine cups."

It is a city in the sands; yet orange and myrtle, oleander and delicate rose, and all the rich-hued blossoms of a tropic land, shower their wealth about it. In the morning the air is heavy with the perfume of blossoms; in the evening the light, to Northern eyes, is intense and enchanting.

Thirty-one miles of picturesque beach are constantly laved by the restless waters. It is only a few steps from an oleander grove to the surf, the shell-strewn strand, and the dunes. The approach from the mainland will instinctively remind the traveler of Venice. A great bridge, two miles in length, connects the islet with the continent. Dismantled fortifications near the bridge show one that the war reached even to the Gulf; and the mass of low-lying, white, balconied houses forms a pleasant group.

Much of the island is unkempt and neglected-looking. Cattle wander freely about. There are a few market-gardens, and some meat-packeries in the suburbs of the city. Galveston itself, however, is as trim and elegant as any town in the South. The business quarter looks quaint and odd to strangers' eyes, because of the many long piers and jetties; the mule-carts, unloading schooners anchored

"The mule-carts, unloading schooners anchored lightly in the shallow waves."

lightly in the shallow waves; and the hosts of slouching darkies, shouting and dancing as they move about their tasks.

The "Strand," the main business thoroughfare, has been twice ruined by fire, but has sprung up again into quite a magnificence of shop and warehouse; and Tremont, and other of the commercial avenues, boast of as substantial structures as grace the elder Northern cities. There is a network of wharves and warehouses, built boldly out into the water, in a manner which recalls Venice even more forcibly than does the approach from the mainland.

The heat is never disagreeably intense in Galveston; a cool breeze blows over the island night and day; and the occasional advent of the yellow-fever — the dread intruder who mows down hundreds of victims — is a mystery. It comes, apparently, upon the wings of the very wind which puts health and life into every vein; and many a midsummer is rendered memorable by its ravages.

Yet there could hardly be imagined a more delightful water-side resort than Galveston, during, at least, four months in the year. My first visit to the beach was in February, and the air of Northern June fanned the waves. The winter months could certainly be delightfully spent in Galveston; and the little city has built a splendid hotel as a seductive bait for travelers.

Galveston is memorable in Texan history as the retreat of the dread pirates of the Gulf — the smugglers and outlaws of Barataria. Though discovered in 1686 by La Salle, it remained uninhabited until 1816, when Lafitte and his pirate brethren from the Louisiana coast tested the capacities of the harbor, and shortly after it was occupied by the forces of the "Mexican Republic." Privateers went out from the bay to cruise against Spanish commerce, and the fleets of Spain were swept from the Gulf.

The island also became a depot for the sale of negroes, to be imported into Louisiana, the native African's market value being one dollar per pound. At one time the followers of "Lafitte, the Galveston buccaneer," numbered a thousand refugees from justice. Lafitte was appointed "governor of the island" by the Mexican authorities, who cared little for the character of their public servants, provided they were efficient.

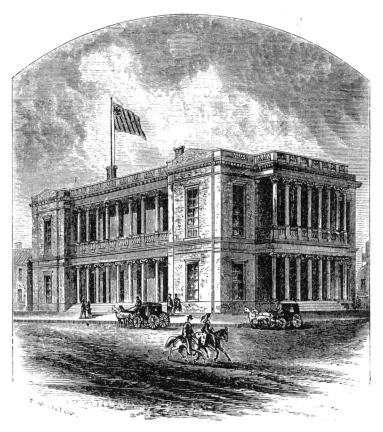

The Custom-House – Galveston.

But in due time the prince of pirates was compelled by the Government of the United States to leave Galveston forever, as his followers had so far forgotten themselves as to plunder American shipping. The island again became a waste, and only an occasional superstitious hunter for the spoils of the pirates visited the sandy shores.

As the Republic of Texas grew in after years, however, so grew Galveston. It was a promising town before the late war, with perhaps ten thousand population. While the rude interior towns were still in their infancy, Galveston was a port of entry, the station of the navies of the little republic, and the scene of many courtly festivities in honor of foreign ambassadors.

During the war its commerce was, of course, utterly broken, and it was occupied in turn by Union and Confederate soldiers. Latterly it has assumed a commercial importance which promises to make it a large and flourishing city, although it has many rivals in the field whence it expects to draw its trade. The cotton factors of the city are enthusiastic in their belief that they shall succeed in bringing to their port the majority of the cotton grown in Texas, but they overlook the formidable rivalry of St. Louis. The capitalists of that city intend to control the whole cotton crop of Northern Texas, bringing it into their market over the new Cairo and Fulton line and over the railroads running through Central Northern Texas; and in case the New Orleans, Mobile and Texas railroad should connect Houston with New Orleans, Houston might take the remainder of the cotton crop, diverting it from the Galveston channel, and throwing it into the New Orleans market. Galveston has but one railroad exit, the line leading to Houston, where all the railroads of the grand new system will centre. Although the business men of Galveston are confident that the cotton crop will all fall into their hands, those of Houston think differently. Galveston has many huge cotton presses, in whose sheds thousands of bales lie stored.

It is to be hoped that such a large proportion of the twenty millions of acres of cotton-bearing lands in Texas will speedily come under cultivation that all the channels of trade will be filled to repletion. The freed negroes, who are throughout Texas an industrious and prosperous class, although, of course, characterized by the failings of their race, and the crudities consequent on their sudden change of station, are extensively engaged in the culture of cotton. The negro who is fortunate enough to have secured a tract of land, grows all the cotton he can, and if he would take the necessary pains to clean and prepare it, would soon enrich himself in the profitable culture.

The lands at the head of Galveston Bay, and on the adjoining San Jacinto Bay, as well as all the lands in immediate proximity to the Gulf, are well adapted to the culture of sea-island cotton — equal in quality to the best grown upon the islands along the South Carolina and Georgia coasts. It would be difficult to imagine a better paying culture than that of this excellent staple, the yield

"Galveston has many huge cotton presses."

being from $200 to $300 in gold per acre. The alluvial lands along the Gulf demand the presence of the China-man; great fortunes lie hidden in their flats.

The export of sea-island cotton is trivial as yet, but growing daily. In 1870 the exports amounted to $17,719; in 1871, to $44,863, and in 1872, to $84,437. Some of the exports of the ordinary upland cotton from Galveston since the war are shown in the appended table:

Year.	Bales.	Dollars.
1866	16,417	$2,146,224
1867	66,271	6,730,257
1868	87,794	7,687,464
1869	84,485	9,997,661
1870	144,123	14,476,550
1871	233,737	16,060,794
1872	186,073	11,898,870
1873	333,502	32,423,806

The commercial year begins May 1st.

The total amount of dutiable and free imports for each year since the re-establishment of business, May 1st,

1866, in the Galveston Custom-House, until December 31st, 1872, is as follows: 1866, $366,388; in 1867, $766,627; in 1868, $251,052; in 1869, $276,588; in 1870, $774,918; in 1871, $1,586,408; and in 1872, $1,940,292.

The number of entrances of foreign and coastwise vessels in Galveston harbor yearly varies from 700 to 1,400. Steamships loaded with cotton run regularly between Galveston and Liverpool; and, returning, bring out English, Irish, and Scotch emigrants, giving them credit for their passage-money, and binding them by contract to work for a fixed sum for a certain term after their arrival in Texas. This plan has thus far succeeded admirably, and is bringing hundreds of worthy families from the slums of English cities into the inspiring atmosphere of the Texan uplands. The main shipments of cotton are, of course, to Liverpool although London, Bremen, and Hamburg receive some of the crop.

There are now fifteen steamers running to Berwick's Bay; eight to New York; a line to Baltimore; bayou steamers to Houston, and river steamers from the Trinity and the Brazos. The steamship line between New York and Galveston carries about ninety-five per cent of all the merchandise sent into Texas from New York, Philadelphia, Boston and Baltimore. The foreign trade of the port is increasing with wonderful rapidity; tallow and cotton-seed oil-cake are important exports; and on my second visit to Galveston I saw the famous steamer "Hornet" loading with cattle for Havana. It is proposed to supply the West Indian market hereafter entirely with Texan cattle, the transit requiring only three days; and there are large exports of hides and wool.

The imports are salt, coffee, crockery, iron and tin, and best of all — though non-dutiable — a steady current of sturdy Germans, who tame the wildness of Texas faster than the natives themselves can do it. Galveston is likely to remain the best coffee market in the United States. The importation of lumber from Florida, Louisiana, and Northern ports, employs a large number of vessels yearly, for Galveston stands in a timberless region; there is not an acre of forest land for miles on miles around.

Thus much for the present commerce of Galveston;

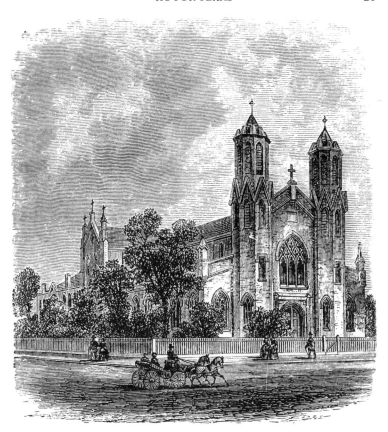

The Catholic Cathedral – Galveston.

its future would be perfectly certain were it not for the rivalry forced upon neighboring towns by the marvelously rapid development of transit lines. Very little fear have the Galvestonians, the cheery "sand-crabs," as the people of Houston affectionately call them, of being "left out in the cold." And they go on building superb new avenues, planting their oleanders, and trellising their roses, without any worry for the morrow. The rebound since the war has certainly been surprising. Galveston was almost depopulated at the close of the great struggle, hardly two thousand people remaining there. Let us take a picture or two from the life of the "Island City."

Morning: A bright sunlight on the silver-rippling water, and one catches the inspiring breath of the waves. Yonder is a mass of dense foliage, from whose green peer out faintest red and purest white, the color of the blossoms and the gleam of the house-walls. Here the oleanders have arched their boughs and made a shaded walk, the magnolia towers above a little balconied cottage, on whose gate a couple of half-naked negro children are swinging; a mocking-bird is imitating the strange whir of the insect-life about him; there is very little din or rattle of carriages or drays; the town seems to have wakened lazily, and to be lolling in the sun-bath, and rejoicing in the hints of the

"Salt and spume o' the sea"

which drift lightly inland.

At the doors of the Custom-House half-a-dozen negroes are lying with their heads upon the broad steps, yawning and joking; at the long, white-painted market-sheds, the market-men and women have done their shouting, and relapsed into a kind of contented rest as they feel the day's heat coming on; under the wooden awnings in the principal avenues of lighter trade a few black-robed, dark-eyed ladies pass quietly to and fro; and from the sea drifts up the chant of dusky watermen loading their mule-carts.

Noon: From this balcony we can overlook the jail, the cathedral, and the town beyond. Primitive enough is this Texan jail — a common two-story brick structure — surrounded with a high wall, garnished with cruel glass, set in cement. In the jail-yard you may see still life — very still life. The jailer has just let the prisoners out from their steaming ovens, and they are stretched on the scant grass, a motley crew — an old man, with a hang-dog look, and eyes which seem to fear any one's face as he blinks in the sun's glare; a frowsy, mean negro girl, slouched down upon a water-butt, smoking a corn-cob pipe; and half-a-dozen stout black men, hideous in rags and dirt.

At the jail's front there is a little tower and a kind of mediaeval gate, where the prisoners sometimes huddle to watch a passing circus or to note the advent of a new prisoner. Invitingly near stands the Court-House, whence now and then issue legal-looking gentlemen, furiously masticating tobacco.

"Primitive enough in this Texan jail."

Beyond the Cathedral, with its graceful group of roofs, there is a stretch of dusty roadway, and, farther still, a herd of young horses quietly feeding. Yon dusky horseman means to bring them in. Ha! Like the wind they fly — every nerve and sinew strained. Escaped? No: The black centaur speeds beyond them like a flash, and the homeward race begins — wild but decisive. Here and there dead cattle lie scattered. Here is the very aspect of the San Antonio plains within a mile of the principal seaport of Texas.

Evening: The tide is out, and you may promenade the Gulf shore along a hard, unyielding track left by the receded water, and watch the negro fisherman as he throws his line horizonward, to see it swirl and fall in the retreating surf to come up laden with scaly treasure. The blue of the water, the dark of the seemingly endless strip of beach, the faint crimson, or the purple, or the gold of the sunset sky, form delicious contrasts. A few sails steal seaward like unquiet ghosts; miles away, at a rugged promontory, where the tide is beginning to set about and come in again, the sky seems to have come down to kiss the sea, so exquisitely do colors of heaven and water blend; the long line of carriages hurries cityward; lights seem to spring from the very bosom of the sea, so low and trustingly does the little islet-town lie on the Gulf's surface; the orange-trees and the fig-shrubs send forth a delicate perfume in the cool air of the twilight.

The depth of water on the various bars at the ports along the Texan coast is so shallow that most of them can never receive the largest shipping; but the plan of Captain Howells, the department engineer, for the improvement of the entrance to Galveston Bay, is an excellent one, and contemplates the admission of vessels drawing eighteen feet of water.

The merchants of Galveston will hardly be contented until they have Liverpool ships of largest draught at their very docks. They have built a wharf railroad which enables the loading of vessels directly from the cars, avoiding tedious transfers. They are also planning for a canal to connect the Rio Grande with the Mississippi. This canal would be of immense advantage to South-western Louisiana and South-eastern Texas; and it is estimated that it would bring into cultivation nearly 4,000,000 acres of land adapted to the raising of sea-island cotton. But this is one of the measures which will probably come with the "moving of the Mexican frontier."

Society in Galveston is good, cultured and refined; and the standard of education is excellent, judging from the large number of institutions of learning in the city. The Collegiate Institution, the Catholic College, the Convent for Women, the Galveston Female Seminary, the Medical College, and several German schools, all have fine reputations. The new Methodist and Episcopal churches, and the Cathedral are the finest religious edifices in the State.

On Tremont street stands the beautiful Opera House, where is also located the office of *The Galveston News.* This paper, founded by Willard Richardson, is by far the ablest Democratic journal in Texas, and takes high rank in the South-west. Its founder has been conspicuous in aiding by word and work, the upbuilding of Texas, and through a long series of years, has published the "Texas Almanac," a voluminous and faithful record of the great commonwealth's progress.

Galveston also has its Club, "The Gulf City," frequented by many of the prominent citizens of the State.

Few cities, with a population of twenty-five or thirty thousand are more spirited; though manufacturing, as a solid basis, is, nevertheless, a supreme need.

"Watch the negro fisherman as he throws his line horizonward."

"There are some notable nooks and bluffs along the bayou."

II

A VISIT TO HOUSTON.

THE need of manufactures is, indeed, strongly felt throughout Texas. In nearly every county farmers and merchants are paying treble and quadruple the prices they can afford to pay for goods brought thousands of miles, whereas, local investment in manufacturing establishments would enable them to multiply facilities for agricultural development, and for the comfort and culture of which the interior is now so barren.

Now that transit facilities have come, such an outgrowth of manufactures may be looked for.

The wheat region of Texas comprehends 40,000 square miles. What millions of barrels of flour, if proper mills were at hand, might be placed in the market two months in advance of consignments from the West!

Houston has already begun the manufacture of cotton cloth, and applicants for situations in the mills are so numerous that the employers are embarrassed by them. At Hempstead, New Braunfels, and the State Penitentiary, this manufacture is prosperous; yet I doubt if more than $1,000,000 is thus invested in the whole State. The people of Texas are learning that they have in their very midst all the elements necessary to support life and make it comfortable and even luxurious; and they are making a genuine effort to secure and hold Northern and Western capital.

In a few years cotton and woolen mills will rapidly multiply in Texas; labor will be cheap, because of the cheapness of provisions and the ease with which life is sustained; and Northern capital will find one of its most profitable fields in the very region which, ten years ago, was hardly counted among the cotton and woolen producing sections of the South. The "cotton train" is already a familiar spectacle on all the great trunk lines. It is carefully guarded against danger from fire by vigilant negroes, and when seen at a distance, crawling across the level lands, looks like some huge reptile, from whose nostrils issue smoke and steam.

Houston is one of the most promising of Texan towns. It lies fifty miles inland from Galveston, on Buffalo Bayou, and is now the central point of a complicated and comprehensive railway system. It was christened after the resolute, strong-hearted and valiant man whose genius so aided in creating an independent Texas, and it cherishes his memory tenderly. It is the ambitious rival of Galveston, and because nature has endowed its streets with unusual capacity for muddiness, Galveston calls its inhabitants "mud-turtles." A free exchange of satiric compliments between the two infant cities is of frequent occurrence.

In the days of the Texan republic, when Houston was the capital, it was an important point. Only fifteen miles below the present town limits, on the banks of the picturesque bayou, that republic was born; for the travail of San Jacinto certainly brought it to the light. Audubon, the naturalist, has left a curious memorial of Houston as it was during the republic. The residence of President Houston was a typical Southern log-cabin, two large frameworks, roofed, and with a wide passage-way between. Audubon found the President dressed in a fancy velvet coat, and trousers trimmed with broad gold lace, and was

"The cotton train is already a familiar spectacle on all the great trunk lines."

"The Head-quarters of the Masonic Lodges of the State."

at once invited to take a drink with him. All the surroundings were uncouth and dirty, in Audubon's eyes; but he did not fail to recognize that the stern men who had planted a liberty pole on that desolate prairie in memory of the battle of San Jacinto would make Texas an autonomy. They did their rough work in their rough way; but it will stand for all time. The old "Capitol," now a hotel, stands on the main street of modern Houston. It is a plain two-story wooden structure, painted white; and contains the "Senate Chamber" which once resounded to the eloquence of the early heroes.

Houston was a little settlement which had sprung up near the town of Harrisburg, the scene of many dramatic events when the republic was struggling with Santa Anna for its life; and the Texan Congress first met there in 1837. There, too, was finally and definitely established the first

Texan newspaper, *The Houston Telegraph,* an adventurous
sheet which had been forced by Mexican invasion to flee
from town to town, until Houston's victory confirmed its
right to live. To-day it is one of the institutions of Texas;
has been edited by men of rare culture; showed wonderful
enterprise in obtaining news during the war of secession,
and is a credit to the State.*

My first visit to Houston was in winter. It was late at
night when, after a long ride from the frontier of the
Indian territory, where snow was still on the ground, I

"Dropt into that magic land."

Stepping from the train, I walked beneath skies which
seemed Italian. The stillness, the warmth, the delicious
dreaminess, the delicate languor were most intoxicating. A
faint breeze, with a hint of perfume in it, came through
the lattice of my window at the hotel. The magnolias sent
their welcome; the roses, the dense beds of fragrant
blossoms, exhaled their greeting. Roses bloom all winter,
and in the early spring and May the gardens are filled with
them.

The bayou which leads from Houston to Galveston,
and is one of the main commercial highways between the
two cities, is overhung by lofty and graceful magnolias;
and in the season of their blossoming, one may sail for
miles along the channel with the heavy, passionate fragrance of the queen flower drifting about him.

Houston is set down upon prairie land; but there are
some notable nooks and bluffs along the bayou, whose
channel barely admits the passage of the great white
steamer which plies to and from the coast. This bayou
Houston hopes one day to widen and dredge all the way to
Galveston; but its prettiness and romance will then be gone.

On the morning of my arrival I was inducted into the
mysteries of a "Norther," which came raving and tearing
over the town, threatening, to my fancy, to demolish even
the housetops. Just previous to the outbreak, the air was

---

*The *Telegraph and Texas Register,* founded at San Felipe by Gail
Borden Jr., Thomas H. Borden, and Joseph Baker in 1835, had been
published in Harrisburg and Columbia before coming to rest in Houston
in the spring of 1837. Three years after its hearty endorsement here, it
quit publication. Although not Texas' first newspaper, the *Telegraph*
was the first to last more than two years.

The New Market – Houston.

clear and the sun was shining, although it was cold, and the wind cut sharply. This "dry Norther" was the revulsion after the calm and sultry atmosphere of the previous day. A cloud-wave, like a warning herald, rose up in the north, and then the Norther himself

"Upon the wings of mighty winds
Came flying all abroad"

It was glorious, exhilarating, and – icy. Suddenly the cloud vanished; only a thin mist remained, and after his brief reign of a brace of hours, the Norther was over. He is the physician of malarious districts, from time to time purging them thoroughly. Sometimes he blows down houses, trees, and fences, forcing the beasts on the plains to huddle together for safety; rarely, however, in his coldest and most blustering moods, bringing the mercury of the thermometer below twenty-five degrees.

Houston is well laid out, and grows rapidly, prosper-

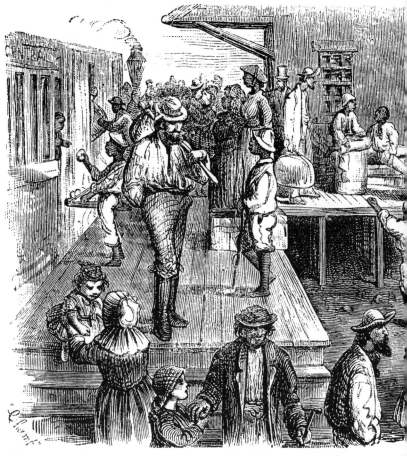

"The railroad depots are everywhere crowded with negroes, immigrants, touris

ous business houses lining its broad Main street. The head-
quarters of the Masonic lodges of the State are there; the
annual State Fair, which brings together thousands of
people from all the counties, every May, is held there; and
the Germans, who are very numerous and well-to-do in the
city, have their Volks-fests and beer-absorbings, when the
city takes on an absolutely Teutonic air.

The colored folk are peaceable and usually well-
behaved; they have had something to do with the city
government during the reconstruction era, and the supervisor of streets, and some members of the city council, at
the time of my sojourn there, were negroes. The railroads
are hastening Houston's prosperity. The quiet inhabitants
who came to the town a quarter of a century ago, and
who, frightened by the fancied perils of the Gulf, have

speculators."

never since been back to "the States," hear of the route from "Houston to St. Louis in sixty hours," with superstitious awe. It opens a new country to them. Northern Texas, even, seems to them like a far-off world. They hardly realize that within twenty-four hours' ride a new Texas is springing up, which, in commercial glory and power, will far surpass the old.

The future commercial importance of Houston can readily be seen by examining its location with regard to railway lines. The Houston and Texas Central connects it by a direct line with Denison in Northern Texas, with the Missouri, Kansas and Texas railway through the Indian Territory and South-western Missouri, and thence by the Missouri Pacific with St. Louis. The Houston and Great Northern route, with which the "International" road has been consolidated (the united lines taking as a new title the "International and Great Northern"), gives a through route from Columbia near the coast to Houston, thence to Palestine and Longview in Northern Texas, and over the "Texas and Pacific," *via* Marshall to Texarkana, on the Arkansas border. There it connects with the new Cairo and Fulton and Iron Mountain route to St. Louis. The Texas and Pacific road also gives it connection with Shreveport and with the road projected from that point across Northern Louisiana to Vicksburg in Mississippi. Houston is

"The ragged urchin with his saucy face."

"The negro on his dray, racing good-humoredly with his fellows."

connected with Galveston by the Galveston, Houston and Henderson road, now under the control of Thomas W. Pierce of Boston, who is also building the Galveston, Harrisburg and San Antonio road, now completed to within forty miles of San Antonio. The extension of the New Orleans, Mobile and Texas railroad through Louisiana to the Texan border will be of immense advantage to Houston.

At the time of my visit there were about 1,100 miles of completed railroad in Texas; and the projected routes, and surveys, indicated a determination to build at least as many more lines, opening up the whole of Northern Louisiana, Texas and Arkansas. Although the roads have been laid down with surprising rapidity, they are generally good, and bright little towns are springing up at all the junctions and termini. The railroad depots are everywhere crowded with negroes, immigrants, tourists, and speculators. The head-quarters of the Houston and Texas Central, and of the International and Great Northern roads, are at Houston. The former route, of which William E. Dodge, of New York, is president, was chartered in 1848, and had built eighty miles of its line before the war. All the rest has been done since 1861, and it now stretches, 340 miles from Houston to the Red river, 115 miles from Hempstead

to Austin, the Texan capital, and 45 miles from Bremond
to Waco, one of the most promising towns of the northern
section. Galusha A. Grow, the noted Pennsylvania politi-
cian, has taken up his abode in Texas, and presides over
the destinies of the International and Great Northern railroad.*

Thus connected with the outer world, Houston
grows daily in commercial importance, and should be
made a prominent manufacturing centre. At present, however, there are only the Eureka and Houston City cotton
mills, running a few thousand spindles; the various railroad
machine and repair shops; a fine new market and opera-
house combined; a few brick yards, beef packeries, and
foundries. In the vicinity, among the pineries along the
bayou, there are numbers of steam saw-mills, which
furnish lumber to be worked into the "saloons," hotels,
and shops of the ambitious new towns in the recently
opened northern region.

There is a frankness and cordiality about the society
of Houston which is refreshing to one coming from the
more precise and cautious East; the manners of the people
are simple, courteous, delightful; there are, in the little
city, many families of culture and social distinction, whose
hospitality renders a sojourn among them memorable. The
Texan of the South is, if possible, possessed of more State
pride than his brother of Northern Texas: he is never tired
of declaiming of the beauties of the climate, and is
extremely sensitive to criticism. Above all, do not tell the
Texan maiden that her land is not the fairest; for the
women of this Southern commonwealth are even more
idolatrous of their beautiful homes than are the men.
There is a touch of defiance in the loving manner with
which they linger over the praise of Texas; they talk best
and look prettiest when they are praising "stars which
Northern skies have never known." They show the same
content with their own section as is found in France, and a
leaning toward incredulity if one speaks of landscapes

*Galusha Aaron Grow was a leading national Democrat of the 1850's
and early 1860's, known for his strong support of homestead legislation. In 1861, as a new Republican, he was elected speaker of the
United States House of Representatives, but was defeated the following
year. For four years (1871-1875) he lived in Texas as president of the
International and Great Northern railroad.

more perfect or of flowers more rare than those of the "Lone Star State!"

The street life is interesting; the negro on his dray, racing good-humoredly with his fellows; the ragged urchin with his saucy face and his bundle of magnolia-blossoms; and the auctioneer's "young man," with mammoth bell and brazen voice, are all interesting types, which, as the reader will observe, the genial and careful artist has faithfully reproduced.

"The auctioneer's young man."

Sam Houston.

III

PICTURES FROM PRISON AND FIELD.

ABOUT fifteen miles from Houston, on the banks of the bayou, and upon a dull, uninteresting plain, is the site of the famous battle of San Jacinto. The character of Houston who fought it, annihilating a Mexican force more than twice as large as his own, and capturing the redoubtable Santa Anna, is, and always will be, the subject of much heated discussion in Texas.

Few men have ever left such firm friends and such implacable enemies. There are two versions of every episode of Texan history with which he was connected, his enemies invariably representing him as a man of bad and designing nature, without special ability, while his friends magnify the real excellence of his character into exalted heroism.

"Sam Houston" was a man of extraordinary merit, sternness, strength of will, and was possessed of a foresight quite beyond the ordinary range. He was a Virginian by birth, the hardy son of hardier and noble parents, going in his youth with his widowed mother to Tennessee, then the boundary between the white man and the Cherokee Indian. His education was slight, and, being refused, when at school, the privilege of learning Greek, which he desired after reading a translation of the Iliad, he swore that he would never recite another lesson, and kept his word.

He crossed the Tennessee river and joined the Indians, remaining with them until his manhood. Some time later he distinguished himself in the war against the Creeks, and in 1823 was elected to Congress from Tennessee. An unfortunate marriage seems finally to have decided his career. While governor of Tennessee, in 1829, he suddenly separated from his newly married wife, resigned his high office, and returned to his friends the Cherokees.

After remaining with them for some years he again mingled with white men, and in 1833, entering Texas politics, leaped to the front, became the commander-in-chief of the Texan armies, and, in the face of the determined opposition of an empire of 8,000,000 people established the independence of the State.

There is but little of interest on the battle-ground of San Jacinto to-day. The ride down the bayou from Houston is delightful; but, arriving at the plain, one sees only a dreary expanse, and the line of rising ground where, on the 21st of April, 1836, the Texans established their camp. On that field, with his little band of war-worn Texans, General Houston made his final stand against the formidable forces of Santa Anna. Suddenly rallying his almost exhausted men, he charged upon the enemy, smote them hip and thigh, trampled them into the morasses and bayous, and terribly avenged the Alamo, and its kindred massacres.

The Texans engaged in the battle numbered 783, and the Mexicans lost 630 killed! The next day Santa Anna was found lying prone in the grass near the field of battle, — his disgraced head covered with a blanket, — and was made prisoner. Texas was effectually wrested from the cruel grasp of Mexico.

Houston possessed remarkable eloquence and great magnetic power. His speech had a certain majesty about it which was in itself convincing to the popular ear. A man of many faults, he was full of the pride and joy of life, although at times intemperate and choleric. There are many traditions in Houston of his fondness for gaming, his adventures after drinking freely, and his power of control over others. When the late war came he stood a magnificent bulwark against the waves of secession and indecision, and always spoke his mind. Never, in the maddest moments, was he denounced; his person and his opinions were held sacred, and he died peacefully at Huntsville before the great struggle was ended. In the various portraits extant of him there is as much difference as in the opinions of his friends and enemies. The most authentic gives him a keen, intellectual face, somewhat softened from its original determination by age and repose, but emphatically a manly and powerful one.

The courtesy of President Grow, of the "International and Great Northern" railroad, placed a special train at the disposition of the artist and myself during our stay in Houston, and we visited the banks of that charming stream, the Trinity river, and the fertile lands beside it; then turning aside to look at the great State Penitentiary, where nearly a thousand convicts are registered, more than half of whom are employed, like galley slaves, as hewers of wood and stone on the railroads and highways.

The sight of the "convict train" is one of the experiences of Texan travel which still clings like a horrid nightmare in my memory. To come upon it suddenly, just at twilight, as I did, at some lonely little station, when the abject, cowering mass of black and white humanity in striped uniform had crouched down upon the platform cars; to see the alert watchmen standing at each end of every car with their hands upon their cocked and pointed rifles; to see the relaxed muscles and despairing faces of the overworked gang, was more than painful.

Once, when we met this train, a gentleman recognized an old servant, and cried out to him, "What, Bill, are you there?" and the only answer was a shrinking of the head, and a dropping of the under jaw in the very paralysis of shame.

The convict labor is contracted for, and is of great value in the building of the railways and the clearing of forests. As a rule, the men are worked from dawn to dark, and then conveyed to some near point, to be locked up in cars or barracks constructed especially for them. They are constantly watched, working or sleeping; and the records of the Penitentiary show many a name against which is written, "Killed while trying to escape."

We frequently passed large gangs of the convicts chopping logs in the forest by the roadside; they were ranged in regular rows, and their axes rose and fell in unison. When they had finished one piece of work, the stern voice of the supervisor called them to another, and they moved silently and sullenly to the indicated task. In

"We frequently passed large gangs of convicts chopping logs in the forest by the roadside

the town where the Penitentiary is located, it is not
unusual to see convicts moving about the streets, engaged
in teaming, carpentry, or mason work; these are commonly
negroes, sent to the Penitentiary for trivial offences, and
denominated "trusties." Sambo and Cuffee have found the
way of the transgressor unduly hard in Texas and most of
the Southern States, since the war liberated them. The
pettiest larceny now entitles them to the State's consideration, and the unlucky blackamoor who is misty as to the
proper ownership of a ragged coat, or a twenty-five cent
scrip, runs risk of the "convict train" for six months or a
year. One good result, however, seems to have followed
this unrelenting severity; you may leave your baggage
unprotected anywhere on the Texas lines of travel, and no
one will disturb it.

A branch line of rail leads from the main trunk of the "International and Great Northern" to the Penitentiary, prettily situated among green fields and pleasant hills. It is vigilantly guarded everywhere by armed men. Inside, the shops are light and cheery, and the men and women, even the "lifers," who have stained their hands with blood, look as contented in the cotton spinning room as the ordinary factory hand does after a few years of eleven hours' toil daily. The prisoners make shoes, clothing, furniture and wagons, weave good cottons and woolens, and it is even proposed to set them at building cars.

The large number of prisoners serving life sentences seemed surprising until, upon looking over the register, we noted the frequency of the crime of murder. The cases of murderous assault — classified under the head of "attempt to kill" — were generally punished by a term of two to five years; never more. At the time of my visit there were seventy persons so sentenced.

Since the passage of the act making the carrying of concealed weapons illegal, these commitments are not so common. Yet the Democratic Legislature last assembled — true to its principle of undoing all which had been done by its Republican predecessors — would gladly have repealed the law.

In a corridor of the Penitentiary I saw a tall, finely-formed man, with bronzed complexion, and long, flowing, brown hair — a man princely in carriage, and on whom even the prison garb seemed elegant. It was Satanta, the chief of the Kiowas, who with his brother chief, Big Tree, is held to account for murder. Being presently introduced to a venerable bigamist who, on account of his smattering of Spanish, was Satanta's interpreter, I was, through this obliging prisoner, presented at court.

Satanta had stepped into the work-room, where he was popularly supposed to labor, although he never performed a stroke of work, and had seated himself on a pile of oakum. His fellow-prisoner explained to Satanta, in Spanish, that I desired to converse with him, whereupon he rose, and suddenly stretching out his hand, gave mine a ponderous grasp, exclaiming as he did so, "How!" He then replied through his interpreter to the few trivial questions I

"Santanta had seated himself on a pile of oakum."

asked, and again sat down, motioning to me to be seated, with as much dignity and grace as though he were a monarch receiving a foreign ambassador. His face was good; but there was a delicate curve of pain at the lips which contrasted oddly with the strong Indian cast of the other features. Although much more than sixty years old, he hardly seemed forty, so erect was he, so elastic and vigorous.

When asked if he ever expected liberation, and what

he would do if it should come, he responded, with the most stoical indifference, *"Quien sabe?"* "Big Tree" was meanwhile briskly at work in another apartment plaiting a chair seat, and vigorously chewing tobacco. His face was clear cut and handsome, his coal black hair swept his shoulders, and he paused only to brush it back, give us a swift glance, and then turn briskly to his plaiting as before. The course pursued toward these Indians seems the proper one; it is only by imposing upon them the penalties to which other residents of the State are subject that they can be taught their obligations.

The Penitentiary in Texas is satisfactorily conducted, being leased from the State by enterprising persons who make it a real industrial school, albeit a severe one. But certain of the jails in the State are a disgrace to civilization, and many intelligent people at Austin spoke with horror of the manner in which criminals were treated in the "black-hole" in that place. All the barbarities of the Middle Ages seemed in force in it.

There is also a certain contempt for the ordinary board or brick county jail, manifested by a class of desperadoes and outlaws, unhappily not yet extinct in the remote sections of the State. During my last visit to Austin, the inhabitants were excited over a daring jail delivery effected in an adjacent county by a band of outlaws. Some of their fellows had been secured, and the outlaws rode to the jail, in broad daylight, attacked it, and rescued the criminals, killing one or two of the defenders, and firing, as a narrator told me, with a touch of enthusiasm in his voice, "about eighty shots in less 'n three minutes." Not long after, tidings were brought us of the descent of an armed body of men upon the jail in Brenham, a large and prosperous town, and the rescue of criminals there.

As a rule, however, such acts of lawless violence are due more to the carelessness of the law officers in securing their prisoners than to any defiance of law. It would be singular if, in a State once so overrun by villains as Texas, there were no defiant rascals still unhung. Governor Davis, in his last annual message, admitted that in four-fifths of the counties the jails were not secure, and that the constant escape of prisoners was made the excuse for a too free exercise of lynch law upon persons accused of offences. He also added that the jails so constructed as to secure the prisoners confined in them were dens unfit for the habitation of wild beasts.

To the credit of Texas, however, it should be said that political bitterness rarely, if ever, has any part in the scenes of violence enacted in certain counties; the rude character of the people, and the slow return to organized society after the war, being the real causes of the troubles in those regions. Under the reconstruction government, law and order had returned, and it is to be hoped that the now dominant legislators will do nothing to hinder their supremacy in the by-ways as well as the highways of the State. The Democratic Legislature can ill afford to undo the wise legislation which established a State police for the arrest and punishment of outlaws, and which forbade the carrying of concealed weapons.

The little towns along the International and Great Northern railroad are as yet very primitive, and constructed upon the same monotonous, stereotyped plan as those on the Red river. From Houston to Palestine the road runs through a country of great possibilities. On all these new lines the picture is very much the same. Let us take one as it looks in the early dawn.

Morning comes sharply on the great plains, and sends a thrill of joy through all nature. The screaming engine frightens from the track a hundred wild-eyed, long-horned cattle that stand for a moment in the swampy pools by the roadside, jutting out their heads, flourishing their tails angrily, and noisily bellowing, as if resenting the impertinence of the flame-breathing iron monster, and then bound away like deer.

On the slope of a little hill stand a dozen horses, gazing naively at the train; a shrill yell from the steam-throttle sends them careering half a mile away, their superb necks extended, their limbs spurning the ground. Behind them gallop a hundred pigs, grimy and fierce, snorting impatiently at being disturbed.

In the distance one can see an adroit horseman lassoing the stupid beef creature which he has marked for slaughter. He drives it a little apart from the herd, and it turns upon him; a quick twirl of his wrist, and he has thrown the deadly noose about its neck; a rapid gallop of a few seconds, and he has tightened the rope. The horse seems to enjoy the sport, bracing himself as the animal makes a few angry struggles, and then gallops rapidly once more away. The poor beef, now in the tortures of suffocation, falls upon his knees and staggers blindly and heavily forward, bellowing hoarsely and brandishing his horns; again he falls headlong; and once more piteously bellows as much as his choked throat will permit. The disturbed herd walk slowly and mournfully away, huddling together as if for protection. At last the horseman, loosening a little the dreadful noose, forces the subdued creature to follow him submissively, and so takes him to the slaughter.

This wonderful expanse of plain, which melts away so delicately into the bright blue of the cloudless sky, has inspiration in it. The men and women whom one meets at the little stations along the road are alert and vigorous; the glow of health is upon them; the very horses are full of life, and gallop briskly, tossing their heads and distending their nostrils.

Every half hour we reach some small town of board shanties, crowned with ambitious signs. Each of these hamlets is increasing weekly by fifties and hundreds in population. As the train passes, the negroes gather in groups to gaze at it until it disappears in the distance. At one lonely little house on the edge of a superb wheat country a group of Germans, newly come, is patiently waiting transportation into the interior. The black-gowned, bare-headed women are hushing the babies and pointing out to each other the beauties of the strange new land.

Not far away is the timber line which marks the course of a little creek, whose romantic banks are fringed with loveliest shrubbery. A log cabin's chimney sends up a blue smoke-wreath, and a tall, angular woman is cutting down the brush near the entrance. A little farther on, half-a-dozen small tents glisten in the morning sun; the occupants have just awoke, and are crawling out to bask in the sunshine and cook their coffee over a fire of twigs. The air is filled with joyous sounds of birds and insects, with the tinkling of bells, with the rustling of leaves, with the rippling of rivulets. One longs to leave the railroad and plunge into the inviting recesses which he imagines must lie within reach.

The Houston and Texas Central railroad route runs through neither a bold nor broken country, but is bordered for at least a hundred miles by exquisite foliage and thickets. At Hearne, 120 miles from Houston, it meets the International line running to Longview, and furnishing the route to Jefferson, at the head of the chain of lakes extending to Shreveport, in Louisiana.

These lakes were formed by the obstructions created by the Red river raft, and Jefferson has become, by the diversion of the waters of this river from their natural channel, the head of navigation in that section. An important steamboat commerce with New Orleans, St. Louis, and Cincinnati has sprung up here, and Jefferson now exports nearly 100,000 bales of cotton annually. Before the Texas Pacific railroad branch from Marshall was completed, 20,000 wagons freighted with cotton yearly entered the town. Though the war found Jefferson a miserable collection of one-story shanties, it is now a city of 10,000 inhabitants, with elegant brick buildings, and a trade of $20,000,000 annually. To what it may grow, now that it is connected with the direct route to St. Louis, and that 15,000 square miles of territory in Northern Texas are opened to settlement, no one can tell. Marshall not only enjoys much the same advantages as Jefferson, but is the head-quarters in Texas of the great Texas and Pacific railway which the famous Scott is stretching across the country to El Paso, and which is already completed beyond Dallas.* The same genius now presides over the destinies of the Transcontinental line, to run through the upper counties from Texarkana to Fort Worth, where the

*Born in Pennsylvania in 1823, Thomas Alexander Scott served as Assistant Quartermaster General on the staff of Major General Joseph Hooker, moving men and material for the Union Army during the Civil War. Later he became president of the Pennsylvania Company, which controlled all Pennsylvania Railroad properties west of Pittsburgh. When the Union Pacific experienced difficulties around 1871, Scott took over its control, later selling his interest to Jay Gould. In 1874 he became president of the entire Pennsylvania railway system. From 1872 until 1880 he doubled as president of the Texas and Pacific Railway Company. Despite the author's bright promise, the Texas and Pacific did not reach Fort Worth until 1876. Five more years and an agreement with Southern Pacific were necessary before El Paso could be reached.

"As the train passes, the negroes gather in groups to gaze at it until it disappears in the distance."

two routes are merged in the main line, which shoots out thence straight to the Mexican frontier.

The International railroad as originally planned was to extend *via* Austin and San Antonio into Mexico; but a Democratic Legislature refused to accord the aid offered by its Republican predecessor.

North-eastern Texas has extensive iron interests, and, throughout the counties in the vicinity of Jefferson, large foundries are grouping villages around them. These beds of iron ore, lying so near the head of steamboat navigation, are destined to an immense development. All the north of the State is rich in minerals.

In the wild Wichita regions, where exploring parties have braved the Indians, there is an immense copper deposit, continuing thence hundreds of miles, even to the Rio Grande. The copper ore from some of the hills has been tested, and will yield fifty-five per cent of metal. Notwithstanding even the expense of transporting ore 500 miles by wagon, the copper mines of Archer County* have proved profitable. All the requisites for building furnaces

*In 1864 some high grade copper was smelted in Archer County, perhaps in part for percussion caps for the Confederate Army. But copper mining did not prove commercial, and was abandoned. In fact, copper production in all of Texas has been insignificant through 1973.

and smelting the ores exist in the immediate vicinity of the deposits. The whole copper region is exquisitely beautiful. The mountains are bold and romantic; the valleys mysterious and picturesque; the plains covered with flowers — and Indians! But who will let the ignoble savage stand in the way of mineral development?

The Indian troubles in North-western Texas are quite as grave as those in the extreme western part of the State. Now and then an adventurous frontiersman is swept down by the remorseless savage, who seems to delight in waiting until his victim fancies he has attained security before murdering him and his family. Government should certainly afford better protection to the settler on the extreme frontier — by some other method if it cannot do it by means of the regular army.

Waco, now a fine town, on a branch of the Texas Central, was once an Indian village, and, long ago, was the scene of a formidable battle between the Wacos and some Cherokee forces. The noble Wacos had acquired, in a surreptitious manner, a good many Cherokee ponies, and, in the pursuit and battle which followed, the Waco village was plundered and burned, and extensive fortifications — traces of which still remain — were heaped with the conquered thieves' dead bodies. Waco, situated on the Brazos river, is to-day a handsome, solidly-built town, possessing many manufacturing establishments. Throughout all the adjacent region stock-raising is fast giving way to agriculture; and great fields of cotton, corn and cane are springing into existence. Every one has heard of Dallas, set down on the banks of the Trinity river, and contributed to by the great feeders of the Texas Central and Texas Pacific. It grows like an enchanted castle in a fairy tale. Dallas is the centre of Northern Texas; has superb water power, and lumber, coffee, iron, lead, and salt fields to draw upon. In the midst of the rich, undulating prairies, and near a plateau covered with noble oaks, elms and cedars, it promises to be beautiful as well as prosperous. It is also one of the centres of the wheat region, some of the finest wheat lands on the continent being in its vicinity. The absolutely best wheat region is said to be in Lamar, Hunt, Kaufman, and Navarro counties.*

*Although wheat production steadily has moved westward and northward in Texas, in the 1860's and 1870's these four counties were important as Texas produced about six million bushels annually.

The eastern corners of the lands now settled in Northern Texas were nearly all held by emigrants from Alabama, Georgia, and Mississippi until the railroad's advent, when the North-westerner joined them in the country, and the Northerner mingled with them in the towns. Slavery flourished there before the war, and the revolution improved neither the negro nor his old master much; so that both are gradually yielding before the new-comers.

In the northern and middle counties, however, slavery never was popular. Some 3,000 families from Indiana and Illinois were introduced into those counties between 1843 and 1854. They owned no slaves and never desired any; and the influence of their example was good even before emancipation came. Hundreds of intelligent and cultured families live there, happy and well-to-do, sowing their wheat and rye in October, and reaping it in June; planting corn in February, to harvest in September; and raising great herds of cattle and horses.

The black, sandy lands are admirably suited for orchards and vineyards; and the "black-waxy," — a rich alluvial, — for all the cereals. As all the cotton lands of Northern Texas will readily produce a bale to the acre, how many years will pass before the cotton crop of the Lone Star State will be 10,000,000 bales?

The labor question is to be an engrossing one in Texas very soon. The proportion of the colored to the entire population being small, the negroes' share in the labor of cultivation is, of course, not large. The Chinaman is already at St. Louis; the completion of the Texas Pacific railroad will establish him along the whole Texan coast. At present, in great numbers of the counties, there is hardly one negro to fifty white people, so that Cuffee stands no whit in the way of John.

With one single field of coal covering 6,000 square miles; with apparently inexhaustible copper and iron stores; with lead and silver mines; with 20,000,000 of acres of cotton-bearing land, and with agricultural resources equal to those of any State in the Union, Texas can enter upon her new career confidently and joyously. As a refuge for the ruined of our last great revolution, she is benefi-

View on the Trinity River.

cent; as an element of greatness in the progress of the
United States. While they vainly court emigration, the tide
flows freely across her borders, and spreads out over her
vast plains. Whatever danger there may be of political
disagreements and disturbances within her limits, nothing
can permanently impede her progress. Lying below the
snow line, she furnishes the best route to the Pacific;
fronting on the Gulf, she will some day have a commercial
navy, whose sails will whiten every European sea.

Few persons who have not visited the South
appreciate the vast extent of territory which the Texas and
Pacific route has opened up. Its most beneficent work will
be the chasing of the Indian from the vicinity of the
"cross-timber" country, which is an excellent location for
small farmers. The settlers there are bravely holding on to
their lands, keeping up a continual warfare with the
redskins, in hopes that they may preserve their lives until
the advent of the rail.

The Indian reserves in this section of the State have, according to the testimony of competent authorities, all been failures, whether considered as protection to the white man or as a means of civilization to the Indian. For ten years the savage has been master of all that part of Texas. The new Pacific route will not only send a civilizing current through there, but will also develop a portion of the great "Staked Plain" territory, now one of the unknown and mysterious regions of Northern Texas. The Transcontinental branch is doing good pioneer work in new counties. It also runs through some of the oldest and most cultured sections of the State.

Clarksville, in Red River county, has long been a centre of intelligence and refinement; it was settled early in 1817, and in 1860 had under cultivation nearly 17,000 acres of corn and 8,000 acres of cotton. It is noteworthy that in this county lands which have been steadily cultivated for fifty years show no depreciation in quality. Paris, a handsome town in Lamar county, is also touched by this line. These towns and counties offer a striking contrast to other portions of the northern section which lie within a day's journey of them. They are like oases, but the rest of the apparent desert is being so rapidly reclaimed, that they will soon be noticeable no longer. By all means let him who wishes to cultivate fruit, cotton, or the cereals in Texas visit these elder counties.

The State Capitol — Austin.

IV

AUSTIN, THE TEXAN CAPITAL
– POLITICS – SCHOOLS.

M Y various journeys to Austin, the capital of Texas, enabled me to judge of its winter and summer aspects, and I do not hesitate to pronounce them both delightful. The town itself is not so interesting at first sight as either Galveston or Houston; but every day adds to the charm which it throws about the visitor. At Austin the peculiarities of Western and Eastern Texas meet and compromise; one sees the wild hunter of the plains and the shrewd business man of the coast side by side in friendly intercourse. The majority of the public buildings are not architecturally fine; the Capitol, the Land Office, the Governor's Mansion, are large and commodious, but not specially interesting. But a touch of the grand old Spanish architecture has crept into the construction of the Insane Asylum, which is built of the soft gray sandstone so abundant in that region; and the edifice, standing in a great park, whose superb trees seem to have been cultured for centuries, rather than to be mere gifts of nature, is very beautiful.

It is, however, overcrowded with unfortunates, and the State's imperative duty is to build another asylum at once. Under the rich glow of the February sun the white walls of the structure formed a delicious contrast to the foliage of the live oaks near at hand, making it seem more like a temple than like the retreat of clouded reason. In wandering through the wards I came suddenly upon a group of idiot girls, seated on benches in a niche before a sunny window. These poor creatures cowered silently –

The State Insane Asylum — Austin.

grimacing now and then — as I stood gazing upon them,
when suddenly one or two of them, doubtless excited by
the presence of a visitor, rose and began dancing and
shrieking. The suddenness of the transition, and the
fearful, mysterious nature of these idiotic saturnalia,
appalled me. I avow that I could hardly drag my limbs to
the door, and when once more in the sunlight I felt as if I
had come from Dante's Hell. The cheery German physician
in charge complained of the overcrowded condition of the
asylum, adding that as the majority of the cases brought
him had already become chronic, it was a hopeless throng
with which he had to deal.

In a yard of the asylum, comfortably inclosed, and
covered by a picturesque roof upon which a vine had been
trained, I saw the sty in which "Queen Elizabeth," a filthy

and dreadful old negress, wallowed all day long. Behind green lattices neatly set into the walls of another building, I could hear the furiously insane groaning and shouting. It is said that there are more than 1,200 insane in the State, for most of whom an asylum is necessary.

Not far from the Lunatic Asylum, in another beautiful nook, is the institution for the blind, which comprises a school for the industrial training of the patients whose vision is hopelessly lost. The Colorado river flows to the westward of Austin, close to the city, issuing from a romantic mountain range, a long gap in which forms what is known as the Colorado Valley; and on the west bank of the river is an efficient and pleasant school and home for the deaf and dumb of the State.

One of the notable sights of Austin, too, is the well-drilled little company of cadets from the "Texas Military Institute," originally located at Bastrop, but now situated on a lovely hill-side near the capital. The school, which is one of general and applied science, is modeled after West Point and the Virginia Military Institute, and can receive

The Texas Military Institute — Austin.

one hundred cadets, whose gray uniformed company is often seen in martial array in the lanes and fields near the town.*

Austin is very prettily set down in an amphitheatre of hills, beyond which rises the blue Colorado range. The little town, which boasts "from 8,000 to 10,000 inhabitants," is very lively during the legislative session. One passenger train daily, each way, connects it with the outer world; beyond are the mesquite-covered plains, and only wagon roads.

The governor, whose term of office lasts four years, has a special mansion, which was the president's house when Austin was the capital of the Texan republic;** and the surroundings of his office at the Capitol are of Spartan plainness. In both the Senate and the House of Representatives I noticed a good deal of the freedom of Western and South-western manners, which would be counted strange in the older States. There were no objections, apparently, to the enjoyment of his cigar by any honorable senator on the floor of the Senate, if the session was not actually in progress; senators sat with their feet upon their desks, and the friendly spittoon handy; but these are eccentricities which prevail in many a State beside Texas. There were men of culture and refinement in the Senate, others who were coarse in manners and dress; the president was amiable and efficient. One or two negroes occupied senatorial chairs, although the Thirteenth Legislature, which I saw, was almost entirely Democratic. The House of Representatives was a sensible, shrewd-looking body of men, with no special Southern type; a Northerner might readily have imagined himself in a New England legislature during the session, save for certain peculiarities of dialect. Here, also, there were negroes, more numerous than in the Senate, and mingling somewhat more freely in the business of the session. The portraits of Austin and Houston looked down benignantly upon the lawgivers.

Texas went through a variety of vexatious trials

---

*Texas Military Institute, originally called Bastrop Military Institute, was founded in 1858 and moved to Austin in June, 1870, where it lasted until 1879, when its president and faculty were employed *in toto* by the new Texas Agricultural and Mechanical College. At least three other schools have operated under the same name.

**Wrong. The Governor's Mansion was built in 1855.

The Governor's Mansion — Austin.

during the period between the close of the war and the election of what is known as the "Davis party." A. J. Hamilton was appointed provisional governor by President Johnson, but surrendered his power in 1866 into the hands of Governor Throckmorton, the successful "Conservative Union" candidate, who was elected after the adoption of a new State constitution by a majority of more than 36,000 votes over E. M. Pease, the "Radical" candidate. The advent of reconstruction brought Texas into the Fifth Military District with Louisiana, and under the control of General Sheridan. In 1867 Governor Throckmorton, who was considered an "obstacle" to reconstruction, was removed, and the defeated candidate Pease made governor in his stead. During his administration, he had a controversy with General Hancock, who had meantime been appointed commander of the district in place of Sheridan, and was prevented from undertaking several arbitrary measures which the military authorities deemed inexpedient at that time.

The new registration which came into force in Texas,

as elsewhere in the South, reduced the number of white voters from 80,000 to a little less than 57,000. A second Constitutional Convention was held in June of 1868, in obedience to an order from the army authorities, then represented by General Rousseau, who succeeded General Hancock in command. This convention was presided over by Edmund J. Davis, an uncompromising loyal man, who had once had a Confederate rope around his neck in war-time. The State was at that time in a very bad condition. Murder and lawlessness were rampant; it was said that there had been nine hundred homicides in the State between 1865 and 1868. The Conservative and Radical wings of the Republican party had much sharp discussion in the convention, which was finally adjourned until the last days of November. Meantime, the differences of opinion between the wings of the party brought forward Mr. Davis as the Radical, and A. J. Hamilton as the Conservative candidate for governor. The constitution was submitted to the people in November, and ratified by more than 67,000 majority. Mr. Davis and his party were at the same time elected to power, and the military force was withdrawn.

Governor Davis certainly succeeded in restoring order and maintaining peace in the State during the four years of his administration, although some of his measures were bitterly opposed. He inaugurated the militia act, which the Democrats of course fought against. It was an act delegating to the governor the power to suspend the laws in disturbed districts, and was perfectly efficient in the only three cases in which it was ever resorted to. During his term, also, the "State Police" — a corps for the maintenance of order throughout the State — was established, and did much to rid Texas of outlaws and murderers.

A tax-payers' convention, held at Austin in September, 1871, united all the elements of opposition against the Davis party. Ex-Governors Throckmorton, Pease and Hamilton participated in it. The Democrats re-organized, and succeeded in securing the Legislature, which is elected annually in Texas. Toward the close of Governor Davis's term, as the tenure of office of some of the State officials was involved in doubt, the Legislature passed an act providing for a general election in December. A new and vehement political contest at once sprang up. The Republicans renominated Governor Davis, and the Democrats, who had been powerfully reinforced by thousands of immigrants from Alabama, Georgia, and other cotton states, put forward Judge Richard Coke as their candidate. In the election which followed, the Democrats elected Judge Coke as governor by more than 40,000 majority; and the State was completely given over to the Conservative element.

This election caused great excitement among the Republicans. Governor Davis, backed up by the declaration of the Supreme Court of the State that the recent election was unconstitutional, at first refused to yield his power, and called on the President for troops to maintain him in office. But the United States declined to interfere; the Democrats took possession of the Capitol; and Governor Davis finally withdrew his opposition. The Democrats propose in due time to hold another Constitutional Convention, and threaten to undo much of the legislation which, under reconstruction and the *regime* of the Radicals, had proved salutary to the State.

On the steps of the Capitol stands the small and unambitious monument built of stone brought from the Alamo. It is but a feeble memorial of one of the most tragic events in American history, to which the State would do well to give lasting commemoration by some stately work in bronze or marble on Alamo plaza, in San Antonio.*

In the office of the Secretary of State at Austin, one may still see the treaties made with France, England, and other nations, when Texas was a republic, when Louis Phillippe was King of the French, and Victoria was young. Three years after Texas had declared her independence of Mexico, the commissioners appointed under President Lamar's Administration selected the present site on the Colorado as the capital, and, in grateful remembrance of

*In 1939 the Alamo finally received a monument, the Alamo Cenotaph, suitable in size and expense. With a sixty-foot shaft on a base forty-feet long and twelve-feet wide, it provokes strong emotions, not all favorable, from viewers. Pompeo Coppini is the sculptor.

the "father of Texas," called it Austin. It seems, indeed, strange that it has not grown to the proportions the commissioners then predicted for it; for the best of building stone and lime and stone-coal abound in the vicinity, and it has an immense and fertile back-country to draw upon. These same commissioners also fondly hoped, by building the town, effectually to close the pass by which Indians and outlaws from Mexico had from time immemorial traveled to and from the Rio Grande and Eastern Texas. In October, 1839, President Lamar's Cabinet occupied Austin — and, although Indian raids in the neighborhood were frequent, the brave little government remained there. Those were great days for Texas — a State with hardly the population of one of her counties to-day, yet holding independent relations with the civilized world.

The European governments had their representatives at the Court of Austin, while hosts of adventurers thronged the Congressional halls. Gayly-uniformed officers of the Texan army and navy abounded; and the United States daily felt the pulse of the people as to annexation. Once in a while there was a diplomatic muddle and consequent great excitement, as when — the owner of some pigs which had been killed for encroaching on the French Minister's premises having abused said minister in rather heated language — Louis Phillippe felt himself insulted, and very nearly ruined the infant republic by preventing it from obtaining what was then known as the "French Loan." *

The Texan government in those early days had always been a great straggler, moving from town to town, and when, in 1842, the Administration proposed to remove the archives to Houston, because a Mexican invasion was feared, the citizens of Austin revolted, and General Houston, the then President, was compelled to leave the records where they were.

In the Secretary of State's office I was shown the original ordinance for the secession of Texas from the Union — a formidable parchment, graced with a long list

---

*This incident is treated in detail in Nancy N. Barker, *The French Legation in Texas*, Vol. I, pp. 209-234. A kind of Chocolate Soldier incident, it was hilarious to everyone except the participants.

The Land Office of Texas — Austin.

of names — and a collection of the newspapers printed in the State during the war, a perusal of which showed that there are several sides to the history of all our battles, and that in those days the Texans were taught that the Confederates invariably won.

The four presidents of the Texan republic, Burnet, Houston, Lamar and Jones, were all strong men, but of widely different character. Lamar was a brilliant writer and talker, clear-headed and accomplished; Jones was an intellectual man, bitter against the Houston party, and to judge from his own memoirs, jealous and irritable. He died by his own hand.

The population of Texas has increased, since its annexation to the Union in 1845, from 150,000 to more than a million of inhabitants. Its principal growth has, of course, been since the war, for before that time Northern Texas was as much a wilderness as is Presidio county to-day. The greatest needs of the State at the present time are more people, and more improvement along the lines of travel. The coarse cookery, bad beds, and villainous liquor-drinking which one now finds in remote towns will

vanish when people and manufactures and inducements to
ease and elegance come in.

A favorable sign on the railroads is the occasional
entrance of some rough fellow into the Pullman car, and
his intense enjoyment of it. I recall now, vividly, the gaunt
drover who went to bed before dark in one of the berths
of a palace car one evening between Austin and
Hempstead. "Never was in one of these tricks befo'," he
said; "I reckon I'll get my money's worth. But look yere,"
he added, to a gentleman near him, confidentially, "if this
train should bust up now, where'd the balance of ye go to,
d'ye reckon?" He appeared to think the berth a special
protective arrangement, and that he was perfectly safe
therein.

The negro and the Mexican are both familiar figures
in Austin, and the negro seems to do well in his free state,
although indulging in all kinds of queer freaks with his
money; he saves nothing. Sometimes he undertakes long
journeys without the slightest idea where he is going, and
finding he has not money enough to return, locates anew.
As a rule, he does not acquire much property, expending
his money on food and raiment — much of the former, and
little of the latter. The commercial travelers in Texas all
carry large stocks of confectionery, with which, when they
fail to tempt Sambo to expend his little hoard in any other
manner, they generally manage to exhaust his means.
There is no idea of economy in the Texan negro's head. On
the Texas railroads, the candy venders are allowed to roam
at large through the trains and practice the old swindle of
prize packages, by which they invariably deplete the
darkey's purse. They display the tempting wares, and hint
at the possibility of gold dollars and greenbacks in the
packages; of course, appetite triumphs, and Sambo falls.

The Land Office is one of the important institutions
of Texas, and a main feature of Austin. The United States
has no government lands in the commonwealth; and the
land system, although somewhat complicated, on account
of the various colonization laws and old titles acquired
under them, is a good one. In the Land Office there is an
experienced corps of men, who have the history of each
county and its records at their fingers' ends, and who can

trace any old title back to its Spanish source. Plans of all the counties, and every homestead on them, are also to be seen. This, in a State where the counties comprise areas of from 900 to 1800 square miles each, is of the utmost importance to persons buying land and wishing to establish a clear title to it; although, as a general rule, the settler who acquires land under the preemption laws of the State, has no trouble, and runs no risk.

An attempt was once made to sectionize all the State public lands — now amounting to nearly 90,000,000 of acres — and to offer them, as the United States does, in open market, but it was thought wiser to continue the original plan. The legislation of Texas favors preemption, and the new settler had best go with it; but he may also become the legal owner of a portion of the public domain by "locating a land certificate," at from thirty-five to sixty-five cents in gold per acre, and then proving his title to it by forming a perfect chain of deeds from the original grantee down to himself. In doing this the facilities afforded by the Land Office are, of course, invaluable. The State Bureau of immigration, located at Galveston, has commissioners constantly in the Southern and Western States, and in Europe, soliciting immigrants to take up the millions of acres in the Western and Northern parts of the State. Judging from the statistics of 1872-3, I should say that fully three thousand persons monthly land at Galveston, coming from the older Southern States. How little we at the North have known, in these last few years, of this great, silent exodus, this rooting up from home and kindred, which the South has seen, and the anguish of which so many brave hearts have felt! But your true American is peripatetic and migratory, so that perhaps the struggle is less intense with him than with the Europeans who crowd our shores.

Texas owes but little money — a trifle more than $1,500,000 — and her taxable property, which was estimated in 1871 at $220,000,000, and was then thought to be undervalued, must now be nearly $300,000,000. In most respects the outlook of the State is exceedingly good; certainly as favorable for immigration as the majority of the States of the West. The grand middle ground, more than 1,000 miles in extent, between the Atlantic and the Pacific, it must be covered with railroads in every direction; and even the barbarity of the savages can last but little longer.

Journalism has had an astonishing growth in Texas since the war. Out of 140 newspapers now printed in the State, 110 have been started since the close of the great struggle. Most of the small new towns have two or three papers each, and support them handsomely. The proprietor of a weekly journal, in one of the mushroom cities, told me that five columns of his paper paid him $6,000 clear profit yearly.

Everybody — merchant, gambler, railroad contractor, clergyman, desperado — patronizes the newspaper, and pays large prices for advertising. The majority of the papers are Democratic, but in the cities the Republicans usually have influential organs. "Democratic" does not always mean a full support of the party, but a kind of independent journalism, to which the air of Texas is more conducive than even that of the North. The *Age* and *Union* in Houston, the *Civilian, Post,* and *Standard* in Galveston, the *Times* in Jefferson, the *Reporter* in Tyler, and the *State Journal, Gazette,* and *Statesman* in Austin, and the *Red River Journal* in Denison, are among the principal newspapers published either daily or tri-weekly. Almost every county has an excellent weekly, filled with enthusiastic editorials on the development of the State, and appeals to the people to appreciate their advantages. The Germans have also established several influential journals both in Western and Eastern Texas; and all of them are very prosperous. In Galveston, Houston, and all the principal towns there are elegantly-appointed German book-stores, whose counters are freighted weekly with the intellectual novelties of the Old Country.

The school question, so seriously and severely disputed in all the Southern States, has created much discussion in Texas; and, indeed, the people do well to occupy themselves with the subject; for it is estimated that in 1873 there were yet in the State 70,895 white, and 150,617 colored persons over ten years of age who could neither read nor write. This appalling per centage of

"The emigrant wagon is a familiar sight there."

ignorance is gradually decreasing under the beneficent workings of the new system, which came in with reconstruction, and to which there was, of course, a vast deal of opposition.

Texas has always been reasonably liberal in matters of education; as early as 1829 the laws of Coahuila and Texas made provisions for schools on the Lancastrian plan; the republic inaugurated the idea of a bureau of education, and its Congress took measures for establishing a State university. After annexation, free public schools were established, and supported by taxation on property. In 1868 the reconstruction convention established a school fund amounting to more than $2,000,000; and in April, 1871, the Legislature passed an Act organizing a system of public free schools, and the schools were begun in September of the same year.

The opposition to them took the form of complaint of the taxes, and in most of the leading cities the courts were overrun with petitions asking that collection of the school tax be restrained. In this manner the progress of the system has been very much embarrassed. The Texan of the old *regime* cannot understand how it is right that he should be taxed for the education of his neighbor's children; neither is he willing to contribute to the fund for educating his former bondsmen.

There have been at different times about 127,000 pupils in the public schools of the State, and the average number taught during the year is 80,000, while the whole number of children in the commonwealth is estimated at 228,355. During the first year of the application of the system, over 6,500 teachers were examined and accepted. The number of colored pupils in the public schools cannot be accurately determined, and mixed schools seem to be nowhere insisted upon. In many counties where the opposition to the payment of the tax was persistent, the schools were forced to close altogether.

In the large towns, as in Houston, the Germans have united with the leading American citizens in inaugurating subscription schools in which the sexes are separated, and have introduced into them some of the best German methods. There has been much objection to the compulsory feature of the free system, parents furiously defending their right to leave their children in ignorance. Texas needs, and intends soon to found, a university and an agricultural college. The latter should be opened at once. There are a good many thriving denominational schools scattered through the counties; the Baptists have universities at Independence and Waco; the Presbyterians at Huntsville; the Lutherans at Columbus; the Methodists at Chappell Hill; and the Odd Fellows have a university at Bryan. Wherever the public school has been established there is a private one which is patronized by all the old settlers, who thus gratify their desire for exclusiveness, and embarrass the growth of the free system.

Between Austin and Hempstead the river Brazos is crossed, and not far from its banks stands the populous and thriving town of Brenham, in Washington county, one of the wealthiest and most thickly settled in the State. The beauty of the famous La Bahia prairie has not been exaggerated; I saw its fertile lands where the great oaks stood up like mammoth sentinels; where the pecan-tree, the pride of Texas, and one of the noblest monarchs of the sylvan creation, spread his broad boughs; where the cotton-wood, the red cedar, and the ash shot up their noble stems; where the magnolia and the holly swore friendship; where the tangled canebrake usurped the soil, and where upon the live oak the grapevine hung lovingly, encircling it with delicate leaves and daintiest tendrils. How fair, too, were the carefully cultivated lands, hedged in with the Osage orange and the rose, the vineyards and the pleasant timber lines along the creeks! What beautiful retreats by the Brazos! One might fancy himself in the heart of the richest farming sections of England. Tobacco, rye, hops, hemp, indigo, flax, cotton, corn, wheat and barley, as well as richest grapes, can be profitably grown; deer bound through the forests, wild turkeys stalk in the thickets, and grouse and quails hide in the bosques. The emigrant wagon is a familiar sight there, and the wanderers from the poorer Southern States find that this rich tract realizes their wildest dreams of Texas. In this section small farms are rapidly increasing in number, land being rented to new-comers unable to buy.

One's senses are soon dulled by satiety. When I first traversed Texas, fresh from the white, snow-covered fields of the North, how strange seemed the great cypresses, hung with bearded moss; the tall grasses rustling so uncannily; the swamps, with their rank luxuriance and thousands of querulous frogs; the clumps of live oaks, and the tangled masses of vines!

But a winter in the South had familiarized me with all these things, and on my return I sought in vain the impressions of my earlier trip. Extraordinary rural charms are like the perfume of the jessamine. At first it intoxicates the senses, but, as familiarity grows, it ceases to attract attention. Even absence will not restore its sweetness and subtlety.

Sunning themselves. — "A group of Mexicans, lounging by a wall."

V

THE TRUTH ABOUT TEXAS –
THE JOURNEY BY STAGE
TO SAN ANTONIO.

GALUSHA A. GROW, once speaker of the national
House of Representatives, and now the energetic
and successful manager of a railroad in the Lone Star State,
has changed the once memorable words, "Go to Texas!"
from a malediction into a beneficent recommendation. The
process was simple: he placed the curt phrase at the head
of one of those flaming posters which railway companies
affect, and associated it with such ideas of lovely climate
and prospective prosperity, that people forthwith began to
demand if it were indeed true that they had for the last
twenty years been fiercely dismissing their enemies into
the very Elysian Fields, instead of hurling them down to
Hades.

The world is beginning to learn something of the fair
land which the adventurous Frenchmen of the seventeenth
century overran, only to have it wrested from them by the
cunning and intrigue of the Spaniard; in which the
Franciscan friars toiled, proselyting Indians, and building
massive garrison missions; which Aaron Burr dreamed of as
his empire of the south-west; and into which the "Republican" army of the North marched, giving presage of future
American domination.

Austin and his brave fellow-colonists rescued Texas
from the suicidal policy of the Mexican Government, and
the younger Austin accepted it as his patrimony, elevating
it from the degraded and useless condition in which the
provincial governors had held it. Under his lead, it spurned

from its side its fellow-slave, Coahuila, and broke its own shackles, throwing them in the Mexican tyrant Guerrero's face; its small but noble band of mighty men making the names of San Felipe, of Goliad, of the Alamo, of Washington, of San Jacinto, immortal.*

It crushed the might of Santa Anna, the Napoleon of the West; it wrested its freedom from the hard hands of an unforgiving foe, and maintained it, as an isolated republic, commanding the sympathy and respect of the world; it placed the names of Houston, of Travis, of Fannin, of Bowie, of Milam, of Crockett, upon the roll of American heroes and faithful soldiers, and brought to the United States a marriage-gift of two hundred and thirty-seven thousand square miles of fertile land.**

The world is beginning to know something of this gigantic south-western commonwealth which can nourish a population of 50,000,000; whose climate is as charming as that of Italy; whose roses bloom and whose birds sing all winter long; whose soil can yield the fruits of all climes, and whose noble coast-line is broken by rivers which have wandered two thousand miles in and out among Texan mountains and over vast Texan plains. It is a region of strange contrasts in peoples and places: you step from the civilization of the railway junction in Denison to the civilization of Mexico of the seventeenth century in certain sections of San Antonio; you find black, sticky land in Northern Texas, incomparably fertile; and sterile plains, which give the cattle but scant living, along the great stretches between the San Antonio and the Rio Grande.

You may ride in one day from odorous, moss-grown forests, where everything is of tropic fullness, into a section where the mesquite and chaparral dot the gaunt prairie here and there; or from the sea-loving populations of Galveston and her thirty-mile beach, to peoples who

---

*Vicente Ramon Guerrero became president of Mexico on April Fool's Day, 1829. Five months later he issued the Guerrero Decree abolishing slavery in Mexico. Texans asked to be exempted, as they felt the decree amounted to confiscation of private property. Although Texans were advised that no change would be made regarding their slaves, they regarded the decree as a continuing threat to their interests.

**For once, the author underestimates. The General Land Office of Texas gives the area in 1971 as 267,339 square miles. Originally, of course, Texas was even larger, as it claimed parts of New Mexico and southern Colorado before yielding those lands to the United States when it entered the Union.

"We encounter wagons drawn by oxen."

have never seen a mast or a wave, and whose main idea of water is that it is something difficult to find and agreeable as a beverage.

The State has been much and unduly maligned; has been made a by-word and reproach, whereas it should be a source of pride and congratulation. It has had the imperfections of a frontier community, but has thrown off the majority of them even while the outer world supposed it to be growing worse and worse. Like some unfamiliar fruit supposed to be bitter and nauseous, it has gone on ripening in obscurity until, bursting its covering, it stands disclosed a thing of passing sweetness, almost beyond price.

Much of the criticism to which Texas has been subjected has come from people very little acquainted with its actual condition. Border tales have been magnified and certified to as literally true. The people of the North and of Europe have been told that the native Texan was a walking armament, and that his only argument was a pistol-shot or the thrust of a bowie-knife. The Texan has been paraded on the English and French stages as a maudlin ruffian, sober only in savagery; and the vulgar gossipings of insincere scribes have been allowed to prejudice hundreds of thousands of people.

Now that the State is bound by iron bands to the United States, now that, under good management and with excellent enterprise, it is assuming its proper place, the truth should be told. Of course, it will be necessary to say some disagreeable things; to make severe strictures upon certain people and classes of people; but that is not, by any means, to condemn the State by wholesale or to write of it in a hostile spirit. The first impression to be corrected

— a very foolish and inexcusably narrow one, which has, nevertheless, taken strong hold upon the popular mind — is, that travel in Texas, for various indefinite reasons, is everywhere unsafe. Nothing could be more erroneous; there is only one section where the least danger may be apprehended, and that is vaguely known as the "Indian country." Hostile Comanches, Lipans, or predatory Kickapoos might rob you of your cherished scalp if you were to venture into their clutches; but in less than three years they will have vanished before the locomotive — or, possibly before the legions of Uncle Sam, who has a pronounced mania for removing his frontier quite back to the mountains of Mexico.

Indeed, this apprehension with regard to safety for life and property in Texas is all the more inexplicable from the very fact that the great mass of the citizens of the State were and are determined to maintain law and order, and to fight with bitter persistence the outlaws who have found their way into the country.

It is true that during the war, and for two years thereafter, things were in lamentable condition. Outlaws and murderers infested the high-roads, robbed remote hamlets, and enacted jail deliveries. There were a thousand murders per year within the State limits; but at the end of the two years the reconstruction government had got well at work, and annihilated the murderers and robbers.

It is a noteworthy fact, too, that the people then murdered were mainly the fellows of the very ruffians who murdered them — shot down in drunken broils, or stabbed in consequence of some thievish quarrel. Of course, innocent people were occasionally plundered and killed; but then, as now, most of the men who "died with their boots on" were professional scoundrels, of whom the world was well rid.

It may with truth be said that there exists in all of the extreme Southern States a class of so-called gentlemen who employ the revolver rather suddenly when they fancy themselves offended, sometimes killing, now and then only frightening an opponent. These people are not, as yet, treated with sufficient rigor in Texan society. There are even instances of men who have killed a number of persons

and are still considered respectable. The courts do not
mete out punishment in such cases with proper severity,
sometimes readily acquitting men who have wantonly and
willfully shot their fellow-creatures on the slightest
provocation.

A correct summary of the present condition of
Texas may, it seems to me, be stated as follows: A
commonwealth of unlimited resources and with unrivaled
climate, inhabited by a brave, impulsive, usually courteous
people, by no means especially bitter on account of the
war, who comprise all grades of society, from the polished
and accomplished scholar, ambassador, and man of large
means, to the rough, unkempt, semi-barbaric tiller of the
soil or herder of cattle, who is content with bitter coffee
and coarse pork for his sustenance, and with a low cabin,
surrounded with a scraggy rail fence, for his home.

The more ambitious and cultured of the native
Texans have cordially joined with the newly-come
Northerners and Europeans in making improvements, in
toning up society in some places, and toning it down in
others; in endeavoring to compass wise legislation with
regard to the distribution of lands, and the complete
control of even the remote sections of the State by the
usual machinery of courts and officials; and in the binding
together and consolidation of the interests of the various
sections by the rapid increase of railway lines.

It was a charming morning in April that I climbed to
the high box-seat by the driver of the San Antonio stage,
and sat perched above four sleek and strong horses in front
of the Raymond House, at Austin, the Texan capital.

Heavy heat was coming with the growing day; the
hard, white roads glistened under the fervid sun, and the
patches of live oak stood out in bold relief against a
cloudless sky. The shopkeepers were lolling under their
awnings, in lazy enjoyment of the restful morning, and a
group of Mexicans, lounging by a wall, cast wild glances at
us from beneath their broad sombreros and their tangled
and matted black hair. In the distance, Mount Bonnell
showed a fragment of its rock-strewn summit, and white
stone houses peered from the dark green of the foliage,
while the State House, crowning a high knoll, and flanked

on either side by the Land Office and the Governor's Mansion, hid from us the view of the rich plain, extending back to the bases of the hills which form an amphitheatre in whose midst Austin is prettily set down.

Nine inside and three outside. "Now, then, driver, are you ready? Here is your way-bill; here are half-a-dozen mail bags; ballast up carefully, or you will have your coach upset!" The driver, a nut-brown man, handsome and alert withal, clad in blue overalls, velvet coat, and black slouch hat, springs lightly into his seat, cracks his long whip-lash, and we plunge away toward the steep banks of the Colorado, bound for an eighty-mile stage ride to the venerable and picturesque city of San Antonio.

Rattle! we are at the bank, and must all dismount to walk down the declivity, and cross the almost waterless river channel on a pontoon bridge. We toil painfully across a sandy waste, and then up the bank on the other side, turning to look at the town behind us, while the horses pant below.

A cavalcade of hunters passes us, mounted on lithe little horses and grave, sure-footed mules, returning toward Austin. The men are brown with the sun, and carry rifles poised across their high-peaked Mexican saddles. Their limbs are cased in undressed skin leggings, and their heads are covered with broad hats, entwined with silver braids. Each man bows courteously, and all canter briskly down to the stream.

Mounting once more to our perches, beside the driver, artist and writer alike are inspired by the beauty of the long stretch of dark highway, bordered and covered with huge live oaks, or with the wayward mesquite, whose branches are a perpetual danger to the heads of outside passengers.

The driver nervously inspects us; then lights a cigar, and, in a gentle voice, appeals to his horses with: "Git up, ye saddle critturs!" — evidently a mild reproach. The saddle critturs dash forward at a rapid gait. Each glossy flank is branded with the name by which the animal is known; and whenever a leader lags or a wheel horse shows a disposition to be skittish, the loud voice says, "You Pete!" or "Oh Mary!" and Pete and Mary alike prick up

"Here and there we pass a hunter's camp."

their pretty ears with new energy. The driver's tones never rise beyond entreaty or derision; and the animals seem to feel each stricture upon their conduct keenly.

So we hasten on, past pretty farm-houses with neat yards, where four-year-old boys are galloping on frisky horses, or driving the cattle or sheep afield; past the suburbs of Austin, and out into the open country, until we have left all houses behind, and only encounter from time to time wagons, drawn by oxen, and loaded with barrels and boxes, with lumber and iron, toiling at the rate of twenty miles a day toward the West. Behind each of the wagons marches a tough little horse, neatly saddled; and a forlorn dog with a general air of wolfishness about him, and showing his teeth as we dash past, brings up the rear.

Presently the driver turns to us with, "I'm a dreadful good hand to talk, if ye've got any cigars." Then, in another breath, "From New York, hey? Ain't ye afraid to come away out here alone?" (Implying a scorn for the outside impression of Texan travel.) A moment after, in a

tone of infinite compassion, as if regarding Gotham as a
place to be pitied, driver adds:

"Wal, I s'pose thar are some good souls thar"
(confidentially); "I've hauled more 'n two thousand o'
them New Yorkers over to San Anton within the last year.
Heap o' baggage. We told one young feller on the box here,
one day, lots of Injun stories, just as it was gittin dark.
Reckon he wasn't much afeared. Oh, no!" Suppressed
merriment lurking in the handsome brown face. "You
Pete! you ain't fit for chasin' Injuns! Git up!"

San Antonio is 2,270 miles from New York by
present lines of rail and stage, and is situated in one of the
garden spots of South-western Texas. To the newly-arrived
Northerner, Galveston certainly seems the ultima-antipode
of Gotham; but once across the Brozos and the Colorado,
and well into the fertile plains and among the glorious
prairies of Western and South-western Texas, the sense of
remoteness, of utter contrast, is a thousand-fold more
impressive. To think, while clinging to the swaying stage-
seat, that one may journey on in this pleasant way for
eight hundred miles still within Texan limits, gives, more-
over, a grand idea of the great State's extent.

Whirling thus, hour by hour, away from railroads,
from houses, taverns, and bridges, and beaver-hatted and
silk-bedizened folk, one cannot resist the growing feeling
that he is in a foreign land, and as he sees the wild-eyed
children staring at him from the fields, or notes the
horseman coursing by, with clang and clatter of spur and
arms, he has a vague expectation that if addressed it will be
in a foreign tongue.

A halt: — at a small stone house, through whose
open door one sees a curious blending of country-store,
farm-house and post-office. Here the mail for the back-
country is delivered. "Morning, Judge," from a lean
by-stander, meditatively chewing tobacco, to an outside
passenger. "Got them radical judges impeached yet?
Driver, won't you bring me a copy of the Texas Almanac
next time you come out? Reckon I kin use it." A drove of
pigs curiously inspect the open entrance to the store,
whereupon two dogs charge them, flank the youngest of
the swine, and teach them manners at the expense of their
ears.

Lime-flavored water is brought in a tin dipper and passed around; such of the passengers as choose, perfume the vessel with a drop of whiskey. "Wal! sha'n't git ye to San Antonio 'fore this time to-morrow, if ye drink the rivers all dry," is the mild remonstrance. As we move off, the driver vouchsafes:

"Thar was Mose — Judge, you remember Mose; he wouldn't let no stranger talk to him, he wouldn't. Crossest man on this line; had a right smart o'swearwords: used 'em mostly to hosses, tho'! Had one horse that was ugly, and always tied his tail to the trace. Outsiders mostly always asked him: 'What do you tie that horse's tail to the trace for?' You oughter hear Mose answer. Took him half an hour to get the swear-words out. One day, a feller from New York went over with Mose, and didn't say a word about the horse's tail all the way to the relay; when they got to the unhitching place, Mose offered the New Yorker half a dollar — 'Stranger,' he says, 'I reckon you've gin me that worth of peace of mind; you are the first man that never asked me nothing about that'ar critter's tail.' "

A ford, the sinuous road leading to the edge of a rapidly-rushing streamlet, on whose banks, among the white stones, lie the skeletons of cattle perished by the wayside! Buzzards hovering groundward indicate some more recent demise. Ah! a poor dog, whose feet no longer wearily plod after the wagon train. The collar is gone from his neck, some lonely man having taken it as a remembrance of his faithful companion.

A mocking-bird sings in some hidden nook; a chaparral cock runs tamely before us, fanning the air with his gray plumes, and gazing curiously at the buzzards. An emigrant wagon is lumbering through the shallow, bluish-green water; the children of yonder grim-bearded father are wading behind it: inside, the mother lies ill on a dirty mattress. Two old chairs, with pots and kettles, a Winchester rifle, a sack of flour, and a roll of canvas, are strung at the wagon's back. The horses display their poor old ribs through their hides, and their tongues protrude under the intense heat.

Our steeds splash through the stream. We come upon a Mexican camp, where a group of lazy peons, who have wandered across from Mexico, braving danger and death daily, have at last found a safe haven. The dingy father sleeps under his little cart. His mules crop the dry grass, tethered near a small, filthy tent, wherein reposes an Indian girl, with a cherub-child's head resting upon her exquisite arm. A gipsy-looking hag is munching dried meat before a little fire where coffee is boiling.

Now along a rolling prairie, in a route disfigured by what is known as the "hog-wallow;" then, up to a range of hills: and *O gioja!* the matchless beauty of a wide expanse of vale below filled with masses of dense foliage, and beyond, forest-clad hills peered down upon by a blue, misty range, far away. A comfortable farm-house crowns the hill up which we climb; shepherds are driving flocks of sheep afield; horsemen are mounting and dismounting; bright-eyed maidens flit about the yard, bareheaded and barearmed; half-naked negro children tumble about on the turf, and little white boys on ponies play at Comanche. Majestic waves of sunlight flit across the valley; the campagna to which we are now coming swims in the delicious effulgence of the perfect Texas April noon. Here and there we pass a hunter's camp. We spin forward merrily, having had plenty of relays of fresh horses, and put the Blanco river behind us almost without wetting their hoofs, so low is it; though in times of freshet it holds the whole country round in terror for weeks.

A halt for dinner, which is served in a long, cool kitchen; a swart girl standing at one end and a swart boy at the other. Each agitates a long stick adorned with strips of paper, and thus a breeze is kept up and the flies are driven off. Buttermilk, corn-bread, excellent meat, and the inevitable coffee are the concomitants of the meal. The landlady stares at the paper-currency offered, as only gold and silver are known in this section. The farmer comes in from the field for his dinner, and his pleasant, homely talk recalls one to America. After all, then, this is not a foreign land. "Stage ready; come, now, if ye want to git anywhar to-night!"

Onward to the San Marcos, another small, but immensely powerful stream, running through rich lands, and passing hard by the prosperous town of San Marcos, the shire of a county whose best products are cotton, corn, and sorghum. The river, which has its source not far from the town, and near the old homestead of Gen. Burleson, the noted Indian fighter,* affords water-power which cannot fail to tempt Northern capital some day. Wood and building-stone of the best quality are abundant; San Marcos may yet be a second Lawrence or Manchester. We pass the court-house and the Coronal Institute; pass the long street lined with pretty dwellings, and ride forward all the hot afternoon towards the Guadalupe.

The fields, in which the corn is already half a foot high, are black; the soil is like fruit-cake. In obscure corners we find little cabins — erected by the Mexicans who abound along the way. Toward sunset we come upon neat stone houses, with quaint German roofs. "Everything Dutch now," ejaculates the driver, and indeed we are about to see what German industry and German thrift have done for Western Texas.

The stage rumbles on through the "lane" which extends for miles on either side of New Braunfels, bounded by fertile, well-fenced, well-cultivated fields, such as the eye of even a New England farmer never rested upon. It is dark as we rattle past the cottages; the German families, mother, father, and the whole gamut of children, from four to fourteen, are coming in from work.

The women have been afield ploughing, with the reins round their necks and the plough handles grasped in their strong hands. Yet they are not uncouth or ungracious; their faces are ruddy; their hair, blown backward by the evening breeze, falls gracefully about their strong shoulders. Surely, this is better than the tenement house in the city!

At last we reach the Comal, and crossing its foamy, greenish-blue waters, rattle on to New Braunfels, the cheery town which the German Immigration Company settled in 1845, and which is now an orderly and wealthy

*The name "Burleson" appears frequently in Texas history. The reference here is undoubtedly to Edward Burleson, a colonel at San Jacinto and later a brigadier general of the Texas militia, as well as a doughty Indian fighter, vice president of the Republic, unsuccessful candidate for president against Anson Jones, and sometimes president pro tempore of various Texas legislatures. He died the day after Christmas in 1851.

"We pass groups of stone houses."

community of 4,000 inhabitants, set down in the midst of
a county which has probably 10,000 residents.

The Germans were the pioneers in this section,
endured many hardships, and had many adventures, many
battles with the Indians, before they were allowed to push
forward from New Braunfels and create other settlements.
As we enter the long main street of the town, the lights
from the cottage doors gleam forth cheerily. The village
maidens are walking two by two with their arms about

each others' waists, and crooning little melodies, and the men are smoking long pipes at the gates. Suddenly we dash up to the hotel, and a pleasant-faced old gentleman, in a square silk cap, hastens to welcome us into a bright room, where little groups of Germans sit ranged about clean tables, drinking their foaming beer from shiniest of glasses. Are we then in Germany? Nay; for supper is spread in yonder hall, and the new driver whom we took up at the last relay is calling upon us, in our English tongue, to make haste.

New Braunfels bears as many evidences of wealth and prosperity as any town in the Middle States. It has always been liberal in sentiment, and for many years boasted of having the only free school in Texas. The shrewd Germans have taken advantage of the admirable water-power of the Comal and Guadalupe, and have established manufactories in the county.

The Comal, one of the most beautiful streams in Texas, gushes out at the foot of a mountain range not far from New Braunfels, from a vast number of springs; and from its sources to its confluence with the Guadalupe, a distance of three miles, has forty feet of fall, and mill-sites enough for a regiment of capitalists. Indeed it is easy to see that the place will, at some future time, become a great manufacturing centre. White labor is easily obtained, and the community is peaceful and law-abiding.

A large cotton factory was established on the Comal some years ago, but was destroyed by an exceptionally disastrous tornado in 1869. There are many water-mills in the county, all engaged in the manufacture of flour for export *via* the port of Indianola, settled by the same immigration company which founded New Braunfels, or *via* Lavaca. The trees along the river and creek bottoms are almost overborne with the mustang grape; the county abounds in fruit, while cotton, corn, and the other cereals are raised in profusion. Irrigation is not difficult.

It is quite dark, and a cool night wind is blowing when we mount once more to the coach-top, and settle ourselves for a ride which will last until two in the morning. The driver cracks his long whip, and we plunge into the darkness. The two great lamps of the coach cast a bright light for twenty feet ahead, and we can see little patches of the landscape, beyond which is the infinite darkness relieved only here and there by the yellow of camp-fires, or by the fitful gleams of the fire-flies. At last we strike across the prairie. The mesquite-trees, which we pass every moment, look white and ghostly in the lamp-light, and flit by us like a legion of restless spirits. Then, too, as the horses trot steadily forward, there is the illusion that we are approaching a great city, so like are the innumerable fire-flies to the gaslights of a metropolis. Now we are in a stable-yard, in the midst of a clump of mesquite and oak-trees; the tired horses are unhitched, fresh ones replace them, and away we go again over the prairies. Presently the architecture changes; the little houses, dimly seen at the roadside, from time to time, are low, flat-roofed, and built of white stone; there are long stone walls, over which foliage scrambles in most picturesque fashion, while, sprinkled in here and there, are the shabby Mexican cottages, with thatched roofs and mud floors. There is a hint of moonlight as we approach the hills, and we can see the cattle in relief against the sky, hundreds of them lying comfortably asleep, or starting up as they hear the rattle of the coach, and brandishing their horns or flourishing their tails. Faster, faster flit the mesquite ghosts; faster fly away the oaks and the chaparral; and faster the little streams which we speed across. Now we mount upon a high table-land, from which we can see, faintly defined in the distance, a range of hills, and can catch a glimpse of the beautiful valley at their feet. The hours pass rapidly by; the night breeze is inspiring, and the driver is singing little songs; we dash into a white town; pass a huge "corral," inside which stand blue army wagons drawn up in line; pass groups of stone houses, then into a long street, thickly lined with dwellings, set down in the midst of delicious gardens; scent the perfume drifting from the flower-beds; climb a little hill, whirl into a Spanish-looking square, and descend, cramped in limb and sore in bone, at the portal of the Menger House, in the good old city of San Antonio, the pearl of Texas.

"The vast pile of ruins known as the San Jose Mission."

VI

AMONG THE OLD SPANISH MISSIONS.

THE great State of Texas is usually spoken of by its inhabitants as divided into eight sections — namely, Northern, Eastern, Middle, Western, Extreme South-western, and North-western Texas, the Mineral Region, and the "Pan Handle." This latter section, which embraces more than 20,000 square miles, is at present inhabited almost entirely by Indians. The mineral region proper, believed to be exceedingly rich in iron and copper ores, comprises 50,000 square miles. The vast section between the San Antonio river and the Rio Grande — as well as the stretch of seven hundred miles of territory between San Antonio and El Paso, on the Mexican frontier, is given up to grazing herds of cattle, horses, and sheep, to the hardy stock-raiser, and to the predatory Indian and Mexican. Across the plains runs the famous "old San Antonio road," which, for 150 years, has been the most romantic route upon the western continent. The highway between Texas and Mexico, what expeditions of war, of plunder, of savage revenge, have traversed it! What heroic soldiers of liberty have lost their lives upon it! What mean and brutal massacres have been perpetrated along its dusty stretches! What ghostly processions of friar and arquebusier, of sandaled Mexican soldier and tawny Comanche; of broad-hatted, buckskin-breeched volunteer for Texan liberty; of gaunt emigrant, or fugitive from justice, with pistols at his belt and a Winchester at his saddle; of Confederate gray and Union blue seem to dance before one's eyes as he rides over it! The romance of the road and of its tributaries is by no means finished; there is every opportunity for the adventurous to throw them-

selves into the midst of danger even within forty miles of
"San Anton," as the Texans lovingly call the old town; and
sometimes in the shape of mounted Indians, the danger
comes galloping into the very suburbs of San Antonio itself.

San Antonio is the only town in the United States
which has a thoroughly European aspect, and, in its older
quarters, is even more like some remote and obscure town
in Spain than like any of the bustling villages of France or
Germany, with which the "grand tour" traveler is familiar.
Once arrived in it, and safely ensconced among the trees
and flowerets on Flores street, or on any of the lovely
avenues which lead from it into the delicious surrounding
country, there seems a barrier let down to shut out the
outer world; the United States is as a strange land.

In San Antonio, too, as in Nantucket, you may hear
people speak of "going to the States," "the news from the
States," etc., with utmost gravity and good faith. The
interests of the section are not so identified with those of
the country to which it belongs as to lead to the same
intense curiosity about American affairs that one finds
manifested in Chicago, St. Louis, and even in Galveston.
People talk more about the cattle-trade, the Mexican
thievery question, the invasion of Mexico by the French,
the prospect of the opening up of silver mines, than of the
rise and fall of the political mercury; and the general
government comes in for consideration and criticism only
when the frontier defenses or the Mexican boundaries are
discussed. "What general was that down yer with Gin'ral
Sherman?" said a man to me at an out-of-the-way town in
Western Texas. "Reckon that was one o' your Northern
gin'rals." As he had no interest in following Cabinet
changes, he had never heard of Secretary Belknap.

Although everything which is brought to San
Antonio from the outer world toils over many miles of
stage or wagon transit, the people are well provided with
literature; but that does not bring them closer to the
United States. Nothing but a railroad ever will; and against
the idea of the railroad soon to reach them the majority of
the elder population rebels. Steaming and snorting engines
to defile the pure air, and disturb the grand serenity of the

vast plains! No, indeed; not if the Mexicans could have their way, the older Mexicans, the apparently immortal old men and women who are preserved in Chili pepper, and who, as their American neighbors say, have been taught that they will have but short shrift when the railways do come. "It will bring you all sorts of epidemics, and all kinds of noxious diseases," they have been told by those interested to prevent the road's building. And this the venerable moneyed Mexicans actually consider a valid reason for opposition, since San Antonio now has the reputation of being the healthiest town on the American continent.

The local proverb says, "If you wish to die here, you must go somewhere else;" and, although the logic is a little mixed, it certainly has a *fond de verite.* For many years consumptives have been straying into San Antonio, apparently upon their very last legs, only to find renewed life and vigor in the superb climate of Western Texas; and so certain are consumptives and other invalids to be cured in the city and the surrounding region, that retreats and quiet residences for people to enshrine themselves in during recovery are going up in all quarters. A few of the golden mornings — a few of the restful evenings, when the odorous shadows come so gently that one cannot detect their approach — and one learns the charm of this delightful corner of the world.

San Antonio is the cradle of Texan liberty. Its streets and the highways leading to it have been drenched with the blood of brave soldiers. Steal out with me into the fields this rosy morning, friends, and here, at the head of the San Antonio river, on this joyous upland, at the foot of the Guadalupe mountains whence flow a thousand sweet springs, and overlooking the old town, hear a bit about its history and the early struggles of the Texans.

France was a great gainer for a short time by the fortunate accident which in 1684 threw De La Salle's fleet into the bay of San Fernando, on the Gulf of Mexico, during his voyage from La Rochelle to take possession of the mouths of the Mississippi in the name of the king of France. De La Salle virtually opened Texas. After he had discovered his error in reckoning, and that he was on new

ground, he established a fort between Velasco and Matagorda; but it was soon after destroyed, and De La Salle's
premature death, at the hands of his quarrelsome and
cowardly associates, greatly retarded the progress of
French discovery. But the expedition, and those which
followed it, caused great alarm, and as much indignation as
alarm, at the Court of Spain. A century and a-half was yet
to elapse ere her feebleness should compel Spain to
abandon a conquest whose advantages she had so abused;
ere she should see herself driven to give up the immense
territory which she had held so long.

Meanwhile De La Salle's expedition caused new
activity in Spain; and in 1691, a governor "of the States of
Coahuila and Texas" was appointed, and with a handful of
soldiers and friars went out to establish missions and
military posts. Colonies were planted on the Red river, on
the Neches, and along the banks of the Guadalupe; but in a
few years they died out. Presently other efforts were made
— the Spaniards meantime keeping up a sharp warfare with
the Indians, the mission of San Juan Bautista, on the right
bank of the Rio Grande, three miles from the river, being
created a *presidio* or garrison, and the "old San Antonio
road" between Texas and Mexico running directly by it.

Meantime the French were vigorously pushing
expeditions forward from the settlements along the Louisiana coast; and so very much in earnest seemed the movements of Crozat, the merchant prince, to whom Louis
XIV. had ceded Louisiana, that the Viceroy of Mexico
began anew measures for establishing missions and garrisons throughout Texas. And so it happened that in 1715,*
after a mission had been established among the Adaes
Indians, and another, the "Dolores," west of the Sabine
river, the fort and mission of San Antonio de Valero was
located on the right bank of the San Pedro river, about
three-fourths of a mile from the site of the present
Catholic Cathedral in San Antonio of to-day.

From this year (1715) may be said to date the
decisive occupancy of Texas by Spain, as opposed to
France; she drove out the French wherever found, opposed
their advances, and finally succeeded in definitely planting
fortified missions at the principal important points. San

*The generally accepted date is 1716.

Antonio was then known as a garrison, and was usually spoken of as the Presidio of Bexar. Indeed, to this day the elder Mexicans living in the surrounding country speak of going *al presidio* (to the garrison) whenever they contemplate a visit to San Antonio. Texas was then known as the "New Phillippines;" and San Antonio, with its five missions, was one of the four garrisons by which it was protected.

The Marquis of Casa Fuerte had long believed that this post would be a good site for a town, and, having asked the Spanish Government to send emigrants there, "thirteen families and two bachelors" (say the ancient town records) arrived from the Canary Islands, and settled on the east side of the San Antonio river, founding a town which they called San Fernando.* To them came sturdy Tlascalans from Mexico, and the colonists built a stout little hamlet around the great square which to-day is known as the "Plaza of the Constitution," or the main square in San Antonio. The town was called San Fernando, in honor of Ferdinand, the then king of Spain. It was rough work to be a colonist in those days, and the Spaniards, friars, soldiers and all, were very glad to get into the great square at night, close the entrance with green hides, set their sentinels on the roofs of the flat houses, and, trembling lest the sound of the war-whoop of the terrible Apaches and Comanches should startle their slumbers, catch a little repose. These Apaches and Comanches overran in those days the country between San Antonio and Santa Fe, and would swoop down upon the infant settlement from their stronghold in the pass of Bandera. They swarmed in the Guadalupe mountains, where even now they come in the full of the moon, searching for horses, as their ancestors did.

In due time, there was a town on either side of the San Antonio river, each with its mission and attendant garrison. Around the mission of the "Alamo" had clustered a little garrison and village. This mission church, whose history is so romantic, was first founded in 1703, in the Rio Grande valley, by Franciscans from Queretaro,

*In 1722 the Marquis de Aguayo proposed to the King of Spain that four hundred families be sent from the Canary Islands, Galicia, or Havana to populate Texas. On March 9, 1731 the first contingent of Canary Islanders, fifty-six strong, arrived at the presidio of San Antonio de Bexar. Their descendants constitute San Antonio's true first families.

under the invocation of San Francisco de Solano; but, water being scarce, was moved back and forth until 1718, when,

"Borne, like Loretto's chapel, thro' the air,"

it migrated to the west bank of the San Pedro river, and remained in that vicinity until, in 1744, it was removed to the high plateau on the east side of the San Antonio, and the foundations of the Church of the Alamo were laid on the very ground where, ninety years after, Travis and his braves fell as only heroes fall.

The mission was known, until 1783, as San Antonio de Valero, in honor of the Marquis of Valero, the then Viceroy of "New Spain." The town below the river retained its name of San Antonio de Bexar.

The missions built up around San Antonio were named respectively La Purissima Concepcion de Acuna, San Juan Campitran, San Francisco de Assissi, and San Jose. The Franciscans, completely estranged from all the ordinary cares and passions of the world by the vows of their order, gave themselves heartily to their work, and vigorously employed the soldiers allotted them by the Government in catching Indians, whom they undertook to civilize. The missions were fortified convent-churches, built in massive and enduring form, and surrounded by high walls, so thick and strong that they could resist all Indian attacks. Within these walls the converted Indians and the missionaries and soldiers gathered whenever a sentinel gave the alarm; and the brawny friars joined with the men-at-arms in fiercely defending the stations where the cross had been planted. The Indians who were induced to settle in the vicinity of the Franciscans, and submit to the religious and industrial training which the friars had prepared for them, were rarely guilty of treachery, and submitted to all the whippings which Mother Church thought good for them. Barefooted, and clad in coarse woolen robes, with the penitential scourge about their waists, the priests wandered among the Indians at the missions, learned their language, and enforced chastity, temperance and obedience. Inside the square which the mission buildings formed were the dwellings allotted both the soldiers and the Indians — the savages chafing under

The old Concepcion Mission near San Antonio — Texas.

this restraint, although they could not doubt the motives of the good fathers in restraining them. But they toiled well in the fields, went meekly to catechism, and were locked up at night, lest they should be led into temptation. Whenever the converts rebelled, there were soldiers enough at hand to subdue them; and the commander of the church garrison was a kind of absolute potentate, who made any and every disposition he pleased of a convert's life and property.

In 1729, the right reverend fathers forming the college of Santa Cruz of Queretaro, were authorized to found three missions on the river San Marcos; and, in 1730, a superior order from the Marquis of Casa Fuerte authorized the foundation of these missions upon the river San Antonio, under certain conditions as to their distance from the San Antonio garrison. The result was that before 1780, four superb mission edifices had been reared, at short distances from each other, and not far from the beautiful San Antonio river.

On the 5th of March, 1731, the foundations of La Purissima Concepcion de Acuna were laid, and, after many vicissitudes and escapes from imminent destruction, it was completed in 1752. For twenty-one years Indians and friars had toiled upon one of the noblest churches ever erected by Catholics in America. To-day it is a ruin, deserted save by an humble German family, who exhibit the time-honored walls to visitors, and till the lands in the vicinity. The San Jose mission, in all respects the finest, was completed in 1771; that of San Juan in 1746; and the "Espada" in 1780.*

As the communities clustered about these missions grew, so grew San Antonio; as they suffered, so it suffered in protecting them. The same Indians who cantered up to the town-gates did not fail to offer some menace to the missions before returning to their mountain fastnesses. In 1758, they went farther, for they assaulted the mission which had been established at San Saba. Pastors and their flocks, as well as the guardian soldiery, were sacrificed. Swarms of the savages surrounded the mission, and the wonderfully rich silver mines which had been developed near it, and not a Spaniard was left alive to bear the news of the dreadful massacre to his trembling comrades at the other missions. Some day the San Saba mines will be re-opened; but their exact location has been long lost to the knowledge of Europeans or Mexicans, and no Indian will point the way to them.

It was sunset, on a beautiful April evening, when I first climbed to the roof of the Concepcion mission. As the day had been heated and dusty in town, I was glad, toward evening, to steal away down the lovely road; past the dense groves and perfumed thickets, along the route which wound among trees and flowers, and fertile fields watered by long canals; past quiet cool yards, in whose shaded seclusion I could catch glimpses of charming cottages and farm-houses, where rosy Germans or lean Americans sat literally under their own "vine and fig-tree."

The carriage rolled suddenly through a ford in the deep, swift stream, came out upon a stretch of open field, and at a distance I saw, peering above some graceful trees, the twin towers of Concepcion — saw them with a thrill of

---

*The author's key word here is "completed," for who can say with certainty when a mission is complete? San Jose, for instance, was established in 1720 and by 1749 was credited as having made the greatest spiritual and temporal progress of any of the Zacatecan missions in Texas. Its present church, however, was begun in 1768.

An old Window in the San Jose Mission.

joy at their beauty and grandeur, just as hundreds of weary travelers across the great plains had doubtless seen them a century ago. In those days they were a welcome sight, for they guaranteed comparative security in a land where nothing was absolutely certain, save death. Approaching, I could see that the towers arose from a massive church of grayish stone, once highly ornate and rich in sculpture and carving, but now much dilapidated. The portal was decayed; the carvings and decorations were obscure; a Spanish inscription told of the founding of the mission. A group of awe-struck girls lingered about the door-way as an old man rehearsed some legend of the place.

The edifice bore here and there hints of the Moorish spirit, the tendency to the arch and vault which one sees so much in Spanish architecture. The great dome, sprung

lightly over the main hall of the church, was a marvel of
precision and beauty. In front, jutting out at the right
hand, a long wall now fallen into decay showed the nature
of the mission's original defenses. This wall was of enormous thickness, and the half-ruined dwellings in its sides
are still visible.

As I wandered about the venerable structure, the
gray walls were bathed in the golden light of the fervid
Southern sunset; numberless doves hovered in and out of
the grand towers; lizards crawled at the walls' base; count-
less thousands of grasshoppers flashing in the air, nestled
on the mission's sides; the stone cross between the twin
towers stood up black against the sky. Curious parapets
along the roof, contrived at once for ornament and shelter,
showed loop-holes for muskets. There were mysterious
entrances in the rear, and the stone threw a dark shadow
upon the short, sparse, sun-dried grass. I tried to call up
the mission fort as it was a century ago, surrounded with
smiling fields, cultivated by patient Indians; with soldiers
at their posts, diligently guarding the approaches; with the
old friars in their coarse robes, building and teaching, and
praying and scourging themselves and the Indians. I
pictured to myself a cavalcade arriving at sunset from a
weary journey; men-at-arms, and gayly-costumed cavaliers
entering the gateway; the clatter of swords and the click of
musket-locks; the echoes of the evening hymn from the
resounding vault of the cathedral; — but the Present, in the
shape of a rail-fence and four excitable dogs anxiously
peering at me from behind it, would obtrude itself, so I
gave meditation the good-by, and asked of the family the
way to the roof.

The barefooted German maiden, naive and bashful,
seemed strangely out of place in the shadows of the
mission. I wandered through the kitchen, an old nook in
the wall, and venturing behind the heels of half a dozen
mules stabled in a niche of the sanctuary, mounted a crazy
ladder leading to the belfry window.

Getting in at the huge opening, I startled the doves,
who flew angrily away, and then clinging to the wall on
one side, I climbed still another flight of stone steps, and
emerged on the roof. A giant piece of masonry, my

masters of today! You can certainly do but little better than did the poor friars and Indians a century ago. Being built of the soft stone of the country, the ruin has crumbled in many places; but it looks as if it might still last for a century. For miles around, the country is naked, save for its straggling growth of mesquite, of cactus, of chaparral; the forest has never reasserted itself since the fathers cultivated the fields; and one can very readily trace the ancient limits.

The grant of the mission of Concepcion was about the first by the Spanish Government in Texas of which there is any record. In March of 1731 the captain commanding at San Antonio went to the newly allotted mission grounds, kindly greeted the Indians who had decided to settle there, and caused the chief of the tribe to go about over the ceded lands, to pull up weeds, turn over stones, and go through all the traditional ceremonials of possession. The same formalities were observed in founding all the missions near San Antonio; the transfer of the lands being made to the Indians, because the Franciscans, on account of their vows, could hold no worldly estate.

We Americans of the present should lean rather kindly toward these old Franciscans, for they were largely instrumental in the work of freeing Texas from the yoke of Spanish and Mexican tyranny. As priests, they were too human and sympathetic to enjoy or sympathize with the brutal policy of Spain; and as sensible men, they had Democratic leanings, doubtless enhanced by the Spartan plainness in which they lived.

The various internal troubles undergone by Spain early in this century had only served to make her more arrogant toward her colonies, and a large party in them was anxious to revolt. At this time there were few Americans in the territory. Now and then the agents of Wilkinson and Burr ran through it, endeavoring to perfect designs for their new South-western Empire; but, besides these ambitious schemers, only desperadoes from the United States entered Texas.

In 1813, however, Augustus W. Magee, a lieutenant in the American army, undertook, in conjunction with a Mexican revolutionist, to conquer Texas to the Rio

Grande, with a view to annexing it to America or Mexico, as circumstances should dictate. He resigned his commission and plunged headlong into the invasion, bringing to it many men and much courage, and fighting a good fight at Nacogdoches; but, finally contemplating a retreat, and unable to carry his men with him in his plans, he is generally believed to have ended his life by his own hands.*

A short time thereafter, the invading Americans and the revolting Mexicans arrived before San Antonio, and attacked the city at once. General Salcedo, the Spaniard commanding, valiantly defended it; but the Americans and Mexicans won, and as the Indians from the missions had joined in, but few prisoners were taken, more than 1,000 Spaniards being killed and wounded. Salcedo and a number of noted Spanish officials were brutally murdered.

A few days later, the Americans and Mexicans were attacked by other Spanish forces, whom they repulsed with great slaughter. But a third Spanish force was sent to San Antonio, and 4,000 men gave battle to 850 Americans and twice as many Mexicans, composing the "Republican Army of the North," near the Medina river. The Spaniards were victorious, and all of the Americans but ninety-three were massacred. A large number of the Americans were shot on the San Antonio road, their cruel captors seating them by tens on timbers placed over newly-dug graves, and thus despatching them. This terrible massacre was known as the "battle of the Medina." Then the brave old town of San Antonio suffered the vengeance of the Spanish authorities. Seven hundred of its best citizens were imprisoned, and 500 of the wives and daughters of the patriots were thrown into filthy dungeons.

From that time forth the history of San Antonio was

---

*Magee, a Bostonian, had finished third in his class at West Point in 1809. Stationed at Natchitoches and smarting over his failure to be promoted, he resigned from the United States Army in 1812 to join with a Mexican revolutionary, Jose Bernardo Maximiliano Gutierrez de Lara, in the Gutierrez-Magee expedition against the Spanish in Texas. Starting with 130 men, they met success at Nacogdoches and encouraged by the merchants back in Natchitoches, enlarged their army to seven hundred men by the time they reached the San Antonio vicinity. After a series of fights from La Bahia northward, the army took San Antonio on April 1, 1813. Magee meanwhile had died the previous February 6. After a cruel execution of Spanish leaders, including Governor Manuel Maria de Salcedo, many Americans "furloughed" themselves back to the United States. Petty intrigues reduced the effectiveness of the remaining army, and on the following August 18 the royalists routed the filibusters at the battle of the Medina river. But though the Spanish forces prevailed, they were never able to silence revolutionary dissent in Texas until the Mexicans established their independence.

one of blood and battle, of siege and slaughter. The Americans, who, in a reckless manner, had given their blood for Texan freedom, were henceforth to act from the simpler motive of self-defense.

The vast pile of ruins known as the San Jose Mission stands in the midst of the plain about four miles westward from San Antonio. Mute, mighty and passing beautiful, it is rapidly decaying.

The Catholic church in Texas, to whom the missions and the mission lands now belong, is too poor to attempt the restoration of this superb edifice which one of the most famous of Parisian architects, in a recent tour through this country, pronounced the finest piece of architecture in the United States. San Jose has more claims to consideration than have the other missions, as the king of Spain sent an architect of rare ability to superintend its erection. This architect, Huizar, finally settled in Texas, where his descendants still live.*

It is impossible to paint in words the grand effect of this imposing yellowish-gray structure, with its belfry, its long ranges of walls with vaulted archways, its rich and quaintly carved windows, its winding stairways, its shaded aisles, rearing itself from the parched lands. As our party entered the rear archways an old, sun-dried Mexican approached, and in a weak voice invited us to enter the church.

The old man and his bronzed wife had placed their household goods in the interior of the edifice; and in the outer porch dried beef was hung over the images of the saints. An umbrella and candlestick graced the christening font. Lighting a corn-shuck cigarette, the old man lay down on one of the beds with a moan, for he was a confirmed invalid. We climbed to the tower, but speedily came down again, as the great dome fell in last year, and the roof is no longer considered safe.

Returning to the shade, the Mexican woman, clad in

*Pedro Huizar was a surveyor who drew plans involving several Texas missions. During the summer of 1794 he directed the survey and distribution of lands at San Jose mission. According to legend, some time after his wife's death in 1798, he fell in love with a choir girl named Rosa. Already employed as a sculptor at the mission, he was fashioning the famous Rose Window when the lass died. Grief-stricken, he dedicated the window to his departed Rosa and spent five years in loving carving of his masterpiece. Less romantic historians, spoilsports always, contend that the window was likely carved by a Franciscan monk, who did it for love of work and God, and not for love of lovely Rosa.

a single coarse garment, her hair falling not ungracefully about a face which, although she must have been fifty, seemed still young, served us with water in a gourd, and then seated herself on the ground with the hens affectionately picking about her. Was she born at the mission? we asked. No, senor; but in San Fernando. And where had she spent her youth? In Piedras Negras, senor. And did she not fear the roof of the old mission might some day fall and crush her? Who knows, senor, she answered, ambiguously; giving that vague shake of the head by which both Spaniards and Mexicans so accurately express profound unconcern. In the shade of some of the great walls were little stone cabins, in which lived other Mexican families. Bronzed children were running about in the sun, and bronzed fathers were working lazily in the field. In the distance, in any direction — chaparral, — mesquite, — cactus, — short, burned grass, and the same prospect all the way to the Rio Grande.

A sun-swept, sun-burnished land; a land of mirages, and long, wearying distances without water; a land of mysterious clumps of foliage, inviting to ambush; where soldiers are always chasing marauding savages whom they rarely catch, and where the Mexican and the Indian together hunt the cattle of the "Gringo;" where little towns cluster trustingly around rough fortresses; where the lonely "ranch" is defended by the brave settler with his "Winchester;" where millions of cattle and thousands of horses and sheep roam fancy free from year to year, their owners only now and then riding in among them to secure the increase; that is the beyond.

The San Juan mission, a little beyond the San Antonio river, some three or four miles farther down, like the Espada, which stands upon the bend in the river still below, is but a ruin. In its day it was very large, and many families lived within its bounds. Now there is little to be seen, except a small chapel and the ruins of the huge walls. A few families live among the *debris,* and there is even a "San Juan Mission Store."

The scene about the humble abodes of the Mexicans, residing in or near these missions, is very uniform. There is a rude water-cart near the door; a few pigs run about the premises, and a hairless Mexican dog watches them; two or

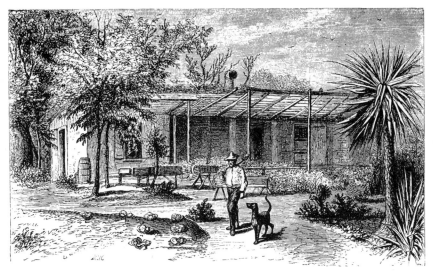

"The comfortable country-house so long occupied by Victor Considerant."

three men, squatted on their haunches, sit blinking in the
sun. No one ever seems to do any work; though the
Mexicans about San Antonio have a good reputation as
laborers.

It was at the Concepcion mission that the patriot
army of Texas assembled in 1835, after the capture of
Goliad; and it was along the river bottom and in the timber
by the river, that a battle was fought in which the Mexicans received severe treatment.

On the river road from San Antonio to Concepcion
stands the comfortable country-house so long occupied by
Victor Considerant, the French free-thinker of the Fourier
type in Texas, lived tranquilly with his family near the old
mission for many years, going to San Antonio now and
then for society, and occupying his leisure with literary
work. A strange man, strongly fixed in his beliefs and
prejudices, he was not thoroughly understood, though
universally respected by the Texans who met him.*

*Victor Prosper Considerant first visited Central and West Texas in
1852 and published his affirmative book, *Au Texas*, two years later.
After sending agents to buy 57,000 acres of land in Texas, he established a colony, Le Reunion, on 2,000 acres near Dallas. Considering
Dallas' current reputation as a stronghold of conservative thinking, it is
ironic that this colony dedicated to co-operative Fourierism should
have existed alongside that future white-collar metropolis. When La
Reunion failed after two years, Considerant moved to San Antonio,
where he lived until 1869, when he returned to France to die in obscurity nearly twenty-five years later.

The San Antonio River — "Its bluish current flows
in a narrow but picturesque channel."

VII

THE PEARL OF THE SOUTH-WEST.

S AN Antonio is watered by two beautiful streams, the San Antonio and the San Pedro, the former running directly through the town's centre. Its bluish current flows in a narrow but picturesque channel between bold and rugged banks in some places, and sloping borders in others, and is everywhere overhung with delicate groupings of foliage. It passes under bridges, by arbors and bathhouses; by flights of stone steps leading up into cool, cozy houses, as the stairways lead from Venetian canals; past little lawns, where the San Antonian loafs at his ease at midday; and on through sweet fields, full of a wealth of blossoms. Nowhere, however, is it so supremely beautiful as at its source, on the high plateau at the foot of the Guadalupe range, where it breaks out from a fine spring, and shapes itself at once into a beautiful stream. Around the natural park of several hundred acres which lies along the base of the mountains, Mr. Brackenridge, the banker,* who purchased the estate, has thrown a protecting wall enclosing a park which an English duke might covet. The stream is a delicious poem written in water on the loveliest of riverbeds, from which mosses, ferns, dreamiest green and faintest crimson, rich opalescent and strong golden hues, peep out. Every few rods there is a waterscape in

*George Washington Brackenridge, a native of Indiana, became one of Texas' leading bankers, merchants, and philanthropists. When Governor James E. Ferguson vetoed the University of Texas' appropriation bill for 1917-1919, Brackenridge offered to underwrite the expenses of the University for the next two years from his own private funds. If he had been forced to do so, it would have taken almost every cent he had. His Brackenridge Park in San Antonio has long been known as one of Texas' and the nation's great city parks. Lately its loving city fathers have won a fight to bisect it with a freeway, so that the patch of Elysium mentioned here and enjoyed for the ensuing 98 years will soon be consigned to history.

miniature — an apotheosis of color. Noble pecans, grand oaks, lofty ashes, shade the stream, which flows down toward a quarry a little above the town, where it again forms a picture such as only the Marne at St. Maur, or the Seine at Marly can rival. To the people of San Antonio it is a perpetual delight, a constant treasure, of which they speak almost reverently. The San Pedro is commonly known as a creek, but has many a beautiful nook along its banks; and in one of them, called "San Pedro Springs," the Germans have established their beer gardens. There, in the long Sunday afternoons, hundreds of families are gathered, drinking beer, listening to music and singing, playing with the fawns, or gazing into the beer garden and the den of the Mexican panther. There, too, the Turnverein takes its exercise; and in a long hall, dozens of children waltz, under the direction of a gray-haired old professor, while two spectacled masters of the violin make music. This is the Sunday rendezvous of great numbers of the citizens of San Antonio, Germans and Americans, and is as merry, as free from vulgarity or quarreling, as any beer garden in Dresden. The German element has been of incalculable value to Western Texas, and especially to San Antonio. It has aided much in building up the material interests of the whole section; has very largely increased the trade of the city; has brought with it conservatism and good sense in manners, so that even a frontier town, eighty miles from any railroad, and not more than thirty miles from Indians, has all the grace and decorum of older societies. The German was a good element, too, when the trying issues of the last war came; and was unwavering in its loyalty. The Germans suffered much, and many were driven out, losing property and money; hundreds were slaughtered in trying to escape to Mexico, or into the North-west; there were shameful massacres; but they were not to be frightened, and they held to their opinions, although often obliged to conceal them.

Texas is a changed place indeed to the people who were afraid to express their views before the war. As a gentleman in San Antonio said to me, "It was like living in an asylum where every one was crazy on one especial subject; you never knew when dangerous paroxysms were

The Source of the San Antonio River.

about to begin." The Texas of twelve years ago, when it was dangerous for a man to be seen reading the *New York Tribune*, and critically perilous for him to be civil to a slave, has passed away, and the Texans themselves are glad that they have awakened from their dream of patriarchal aristocracy, which placed such a check upon the development of the State. The Germans have settled several thriving places west of San Antonio, the most noted of which is Fredericksburg. German and Jewish names are over the doors of certainly more than half the business houses in San Antonio; and German or Hebrew talent conducts many vast establishments which have trade with the surrounding country, or with Mexico.

San Antonio has so long been a depot for military supplies for all the forts on the south-western frontier, and for the Mexican States this side of the Sierra Madre, that some of the merchants are not in favor of the advent of railroads, fearing that with them trade will move beyond the venerable city, and forgetting that even in that event there will be ample compensating advantages. The sooner

Western Texas has railroads, the sooner will the Indian and Mexican difficulties be settled; the sooner will all the available rich lands be taken up. Even now the business done by means of the slow wagon trains, which can at best only make twenty miles per day, is enormous, amounting to many millions yearly. What will it be when railroads penetrate to the now untamed frontiers? Many of the appliances of civilization are fast reaching Western Texas for the first time. San Antonio now has four prosperous banks — she had none before the war — gas-lights, two daily papers, and a weekly for the Germans; how can she avoid railroads?

Three lines are at present pointed directly at the antique city; the Galveston, Harrisburg and San Antonio railroad, nearly completed; the Gulf, Western Texas and Pacific railroad, which at present extends from Indianola to Victoria, and has been graded to Cuero, thirty miles beyond Victoria; and the International railroad, which

San Pedro Springs — "The Germans have established their beer gardens."

"Every few rods there is a waterscape in miniature."

contemplates touching both Austin and San Antonio, thus opening a through line to Longview, in Northern Texas, and south-westward to Mazatlan on the Pacific, with a branch to the city of Mexico. There is not much probability that the last line will be finished to San Antonio, at least for many years.*

The *plazas*, or public squares of San Antonio, merit special attention. The four principal ones are the Alamo, the Constitution, the Military, and Travis. The latter is a handsome grass-grown common surrounded by pretty residences, some of them fronting upon charming lawns and gardens; a stone church is to be erected there by the Episcopalians. The Ursuline Convent and St. Mary's Church are among the noticeable Catholic edifices of the town.

The old church of San Fernando is now removed from the "Plaza of the Constitution," or rather is en-

---

*When the International and Great Northern ceased to be an independent line in 1924, it owned 1,106 miles in Texas, the longest and oldest line in the Missouri Pacific system in Texas. It was also the only Texas railroad to have been exempted from taxes for twenty-five years, with the Texas and Pacific the only line to have received twenty sections of land from the state for each mile of track, as against a maximum of sixteen sections for other roads, and the only railroad providing a Texas governor, Thomas M. Campbell, from the ranks of its general managers. The author is realistic here, as the first passenger train did not reach San Antonio until February 16, 1881.

"The river passes by arbors and bath-houses."

shrined within a new and imposing edifice, built of the
white stone of the section. The Constitution plaza is the
original garrison square of San Fernando, and streets lead
out from it into the open country, the Military place, and
the main part of the town. The Military plaza is surrounded by storehouses and shops, and is always filled
with wagon teams and their picturesque and ragged drivers.
From thence it is only a few steps to one of the Mexican
quarters of the town, sometimes called "Laredito." There
the life of the eighteenth century still prevails, without
taint of modernism. Wandering along the unpaved street in

the evening, one finds the doors of all the Mexican cottages open, and has only to enter and demand supper to be instantly served; for the Mexican has learned to turn American curiosity about his cookery to account. Entering one of these hovels, you will find a long, rough table with wooden benches about it; a single candlestick dimly sending its light into the dark recesses of the unceiled roof; a hard earth-floor, in which the fowls are busily bestowing themselves for sleep; a few dishes arranged on the table, and glasses and coffee-cups beside them. The fat, tawny Mexican *materfamilias* will place before you various savory compounds, swimming in fiery pepper, which biteth like a serpent; and the *tortilla*, a smoking hot cake, thin as a shaving, and about as eatable, is the substitute for bread. This meal, with bitterest of coffee to wash it down, and dulcet Spanish talked by your neighbors at table for dessert, will be an event in your gastronomic experience. You will see many Americans scattered along at the tables in the little houses in Laredito; everywhere I went there was a large party of the curious, ciceroned by one of the oldest and most respected of San Antonio's citizens, "Don Juan" Twohig, the wealthy Irish banker, who was sixty-five years old that very day, but rolled tortillas as heartily

The Ursuline Convent — San Antonio.

St. Mary's Church – San Antonio.

as when a sturdy youth, and was as gay as when, a gallant revolutionist, he beguiled the hours of captivity in the Castle of Perote, where the cruel Mexicans had sent him.*

The residences on Flores street are all completely embowered in shrubbery, and many of them are intrinsically fine. There are few wooden structures in the city. The solid architecture of previous centuries prevails. Putting up a house is a work of time; the Mexicans slowly saw and carve the great stones; but the work is solid when completed, and fire-proof. Most of the houses and blocks in Commerce and other principal streets are two stories high — sometimes three — and there are some fine shops — one or two of them being veritable museums of traffic.

It is from these shops that the assortments are made up which toil across the plains to the garrisons and to Mexico; and a wagon-train, loaded with a "varied assort-

*John Twohig reached San Antonio from Ireland in 1830. When the Mexican general Adrian Woll invaded San Antonio in September 1842, Twohig blew up his store to keep ammunition from the hands of the Mexican army. Held in infamous Perote prison, he and fourteen other San Antonians tunneled their way out the next year. He was one of nine not recaptured. Later, as he grew wealthy, Twohig was famous for his breadline for the poor, which he financed personally. He died in San Antonio in October 1891.

ment," contains almost everything known in trade. Through the narrow streets every day clatter the mule-teams, their tattered and dirty-clothed negro drivers shouting frantically at them as they drag civilized appliances toward Mexico. These wagoners lead a wild life of almost constant danger and adventure, but they are fascinated with it, and can rarely be induced to give it up.

The Mexicans monopolize a corner of the town, which has won the *sobriquet* of "Chihuahua." It is a picturesque collection of hovels, built of logs, stones, and dried mud, and thatched with brush or straw. Little gardens are laid out in front of the houses, some of which are no larger than a sentry-box, and naked children play in the primitive streets. Young girls, bold-eyed and beautiful, gayly dressed, and with shawls thrown lightly over their superb heads, saunter idly about, gossiping, or staring saucily at strangers; the elder women wash clothes by the brookside. The men seem to be perpetually waiting for some one to come and feed them. They wander about in the most purposeless fashion, and one is tempted to think them on the look-out for a chance to rob or murder; yet they are, on the contrary, quite inoffensive. "Chihuahua" and "Laredito" are nooks that one would never suspect could exist on American soil. But the Mexican is hard-headed, and terribly prejudiced; he cannot be made to see that his slow, primitive ways, his filth and lack of comfort, are not better than the frugal decency and careful home management of the Germans and Americans who surround him.

A Mexican Hovel.

The Military Plaza — San Antonio.

The Alamo is the shrine to which every pilgrim to this strange corner of America must do utmost reverence. It is venerable as mission church and fortress, and was so baptized in blood that it is world-famous. The terse inscription on the Alamo monument, in the porch of the capitol at Austin, *"Thermopylae had her messenger of death; the Alamo had none!"* indicates the reverence in which the ruins are held by Texans. There is now but little left of the original edifice. The portion still standing is used as a Government storehouse; and the place where Travis and his immortals fell, which should be the site of a fine monument, is a station for the mule and ox-teams waiting to receive stores.

It was a noteworthy struggle which led to the massacre at the Alamo, and thence to Texan independence. Moses and Stephen F. Austin, father and son, struggled through a dreary period of colonization from 1821 until 1836. The father died before he had succeeded in availing himself, to any extent, of the hesitating permission he had received from the Spaniards to introduce Americans into Texas; but his son took that permission as his patrimony, and went at the work with a will.

"The Mexicans slowly saw and carve the great stones."

"The elder women wash clothes by the brookside."

Stephen Austin was obliged to brave a thousand dangers in founding his first colony on the banks of the Brazos; but the colony grew, and acquired a steadiness and prosperity, even while the adjacent Mexican States were undergoing twenty revolutions. The time, however, came, and speedily, when the Government of Mexico perceived that the two races were radically antagonistic, and that American activity would soon conquer the whole territory, unless force were opposed to it. So, with the usual blindness of despotism, Guerrero, the weak and despicable tyrant, began hostilities against the Americans, and detachments of soldiers crept in upon the colonists, occupying various posts, under one pretext or another, until the colonists saw through the ruse, and openly defied the crafty invaders.

Guerrero continued provocative measures; freeing slaves throughout Mexico, and thus violating a treaty made with the American colonists; and at last the Mexican Congress forbade any more Americans to enter Texas.

Then came the thunder-storm! The colonists sent commissioners to complain to the Mexican Government of their ill-treatment. These commissioners were imprisoned and abused, and the colonists flew to arms — took the citadel of Anahuac — took other fortresses and held them — released their commissioners — repudiated Mexico — met in convention at San Felipe, in 1832, and drew up a constitution under which they desired to live. Stephen

Mexican types in San Antonio.

Austin agreed to present it to the parent government in the city of Mexico, but when he reached that place he was thrown into prison. This and other odious tyrannies of Santa Anna, the new ruler and liberator of Mexico, opened the way to the Alamo, to San Jacinto, and to independence. It was a bloody path, but bravely trod! There were giants in those days, men who gave their lives cheerfully, men who held death in contempt. Such men were Austin, Houston, Travis, Fannin, and Milam.

The final struggle between Santa Anna, dictator of Mexico, and the Texan-American army began in 1834. It was a clever pretext which brought about the real war. The Mexican governor of Coahuila, the province allied to Texas, had, in order to meet his expenses, proposed the sale of lands in Texas.

Numerous speculators presented themselves; but they were all Americans, and when this became known, the Mexican Government refused to ratify the governor's action. The governor insisted; troops were sent into Coahuila to expel the rebel Legislature which had voted the land measure, and the Texan-Americans found themselves, as well as their neighbors, in danger of invasion. They could wait no longer; they raised the standard of revolt on the plains of San Jacinto, August 16, 1835;* and as soon as the news of the rebellion came to Mexican ears, General Cos, by Santa Anna's orders, sat down before San Antonio, the rebellious capital, to starve it into submission. There was fighting everywhere — at Goliad, at Gonzales, in all the towns, and around them.

General Cos took San Antonio; was besieged in it; had to give it up to brave Ben Milam and the "three hundred men who were ready to die;" and, a little time after, the people of Texas, assembled in convention at Washington, on the Brazos river, enthusiastically voted the declaration of the absolute independence of Texas. So Santa Anna, with three army corps, began the third siege of San Antonio.

As you see the remnant of the old fort of the Alamo now, its battered walls looming up without picturesque effect against the brilliant sky, and the clouds of dust which the muleteers and their teams stir up, half hiding it — perhaps it does not seem to you like a grand historic memorial. Indeed it is not so grand as in its old days, when, as a church, standing proudly under the shade of the noble cottonwood trees, it was the cynosure of every eye. It has fallen much into decay, and the Government, which would use Washington's tomb for a storehouse, rather than build a proper one, if Mount Vernon were a military depot, has cumbered it with boxes and barrels.

But you must picture the old fort as it was on Sunday, the 6th of March, 1836, when Texas was a young

*Not clear what he is talking about. The Texas Revolution is generally considered to have begun militarily on October 2, 1835 at Gonzales, and politically with the meeting of the Consultation at San Felipe on October 16, where the decision was taken to remain within Mexican sovereignty under the Constitution of 1824 but to resist General Santa Anna, who had usurped power and therefore temporarily negated that liberal document.

"The remnant of the old fort of the Alamo."

and war-ridden republic. Santa Anna, with an overwhelming force of infantry, had hemmed in and forced to retreat into the fort a little band of one hundred and forty or fifty men,* commanded by Lieutenant-Colonel Travis. In those days the fort extended over two or three acres.

A thousand men would hardly have been sufficient to man the defenses. It was a capacious structure, with chapel, long stone barracks, barrier walls, and intrenchments, fortified with cannon. The barracks were loopholed, and the doors were barricaded with semicircular parapets, made of double curtains of hides filled with earth. The walls were so tremendously thick and strong that batteries playing upon them night and day produced but little effect.

It was a troublous time for the new republic; the United States had given sympathy, but no aid; the Mexican troops were ten times as numerous as were the patroit armies; terrible struggles against the enemy had been made at Goliad, and at other places, but in vain; all hope of succor was cut off from the soldiers in the Alamo, although Houston's little army was doing its best to rally. Fannin was desperately awaiting the attack upon Goliad. The Alamo and its defenders were left alone, to the mercy of the "Napoleon of the West."

But Lieutenant-Colonel Travis and the little garrison had made up their minds. There was but one idea of duty in the souls of these men. Bowie and Crockett and Bonham, and those noble volunteers who had succeeded in making their way into the fort from the town of Gonzales — one hundred and eighty-eight souls in all, say some chroniclers, — resolved to defend the Alamo to the uttermost. Like Leonidas and his Spartans at Thermopylae, they pledged themselves to victory or death. Then and there did they consecrate Texas to liberty. The Alamo was stormed by thousands of ferocious Spaniards and Mexicans. The Texans fought like demons, killing hundreds of their assailants, but were finally overpowered, and were all put to death. Two women, their two children, and a negro boy, were the only survivors of this dreadful massacre; and

*The most generally accepted number of fighting Texans at the Alamo is 187.

but one, a Mexican woman, is alive to-day.* The "Napoleon of the West" gave his name to infamy, and sealed the doom of his own cause by this infamous massacre and the still bloodier one which followed it at Goliad. The heroism of the Alamo was the inspiration of the men who fell upon Santa Anna's army at San Jacinto, destroyed it, and made Texas free. Not even the bones of Travis and his men were preserved. The mutilated bodies were burned a few hours after they fell; and the fierce north winds which now and then sweep over San Antonio, have long ago scattered the ashes which the Texans a year after the massacre had gathered up and reverently buried.

*Doubt remains whether Andrea Castanon Candalaria — Madame Candalaria — was actually in the Alamo attending the ailing James Bowie, as she claimed. But since she outlived the other survivors, no one could say she wasn't, and in 1891 — 56 years after the Battle of the Alamo — the Texas legislature voted her a pension of $12 a month until she died on February 10, 1899 at 113 years of age.

A Texan Cattle-Drover.

VIII

THE PLAINS – THE CATTLE TRADE.

THERE are many almost distinctively Mexican types to be seen in the San Antonio streets. Prominent among them are the horsemen from the plains, with their blankets well girt about them, and their swarthy features shaded by broadest of sombreros. Youths mounted on overloaded little mules shout lustily in Spanish. The drivers of the ox-teams swear and swear again as they crack their long whips, and groups of rough, semi-Indian looking men sun themselves at unprotected corners. The candy and fruit merchants lazily wave their fly-brushes, and sit staring open-eyed all day, although the intense sunlight reflected from the hard, white roads is painfully annoying to the stranger. The old beggars, half-blind and wholly ragged, huddle together, howling for alms, and invoking ten thousand saints, or, muttering to themselves, stray aimlessly up and down the avenues.

A residence of a few weeks in San Antonio affords one a good look into the cattle trade of Western Texas, one of the most remarkable industries of the southwest. One might with justice call it an indolent industry – for it accomplishes great results in a lazy, disorderly way, and makes men millionaires before they have had time to arouse themselves for real work.

Cattle-trading is a grand pastime with hundreds of Texans. They like the grandiloquent sound of a "purchase of 60,000 head." There is something at once princely and patriarchal about it. They enjoy the adventurous life on the great grazing plains, the freedom of the ranch, the possibility of an Indian incursion, the swift coursing on

"The horsemen from the plains."

horseback over the great stretches, the romance of the road. Nearly all the immense region from the Colorado to the Rio Grande is given up to stock-raising. The mesquite grass carpets the plains from end to end, and the horses, cattle and sheep luxuriate in it; while the giant pecan throws down stores of oily nuts every year for the wandering hogs to revel over.

The mountainous regions around San Antonio offer superb facilities for sheep husbandry; and the valleys along the streams are fertile enough for the most exacting farmer. There are millions of cattle now scattered over the plains between San Antonio and the Rio Grande, and the number is steadily increasing. It is not uncommon for a single individual to own 200,000 head.*

The cattle owners of Western Texas have been much before the public for the last few years, on account of their numerous complaints of thievery on the frontier.

*Anyone owning 200,000 head of cattle is uncommon, whether the year be 1874 or 1974.

While I was in San Antonio a Government commission arrived from a long and tedious journey through the Rio Grande valley and the country between San Antonio and the Mexican boundary, where they had been taking testimony with regard to the Mexican outrages.

Opinion seems somewhat divided as to the extent and nature of the damage done the cattle-raising interest by the Mexicans, some Texans even asserting that the Texan claims are grossly exaggerated, and that there has been much stealing on both sides of the Rio Grande. But the commission itself has taken testimony with great care, and, whatever may be the exact nature of the claims against Mexico, they are enough to justify a prompt aggressive policy in case the hybrid neighbor republic does not see fit to take notice of the demands of her more powerful sister. The troubles on the Mexican-Texan frontier have resulted largely from an attack made on the Kickapoo Indians. It appears that these Indians, during our late civil war, left their reservation with the intention of going to Mexico, and while passing through Texas in May of 1864,

"The candy and fruit merchants lazily wave their fly-brushes."

were mistaken for a hostile force by a Confederate corps of observation, and were attacked.* When the mistake was corrected, the Indians were allowed to proceed on their way; but they found the attack a pretext for an offensive policy, and soon after reaching Mexico began a series of distressing frontier depredations. There were only nine hundred and thirty-five of these Kickapoo Indians, originally; and it is now supposed that at least half of them are dead; but those who remain are terrible fellows. The Kickapoo is a kind of perverted Indian; he is unlike the original tribes of Texas, who, like their neighbors in Mexico, were mild-mannered until aroused by ideas of wrong. He was born with the genius of murder and rapine firmly implanted in his breast, and being somewhat civilized, of course he is much worse than if he were a pure savage. He had not been long in Mexico before he began to dominate the native Mexican Indians; and the Comanches joining with them, they soon had things their own way in their new home.

These Bedouins of the West have been a terror to the stock-farmer since 1864. They have acted like fiends; seeming to be far more malignant and savage than their ancestors. Indeed, as the Indian race decreases in Texas, from disease, internal dissensions, and intangible causes, the "type of the decadence" is the most repulsive which the blood has ever produced. It is as if the savage spirit made its last protest against annihilation tenfold more bitter and deadly than its first.

The Kickapoos, in conjunction with Comanches, Apaches, and Mexicans, have carried off immense herds, and committed numberless murders. They have been almost ubiquitous, overrunning that vast section between the Rio Grande and San Antonio rivers, and the road

---

**The author probably means the Battle of Dove Creek, sixteen miles south of San Angelo, on January 8, 1865. Three hundred seventy state border guards overtook fourteen hundred Kickapoo. The Texans lost thirty-six killed and sixty wounded, while the Indians lost eleven men, with thirty-one wounded. The Kickapoo continued to Mexico, while the Texans retreated to the Colorado river. On the other hand, Confederate forces did massacre a small band of German Unionists who were trying to make their way from their Hill Country homes to Mexico in August 1862. Two months later they caught up with thirty-seven escapees, and killed six more of them. Of the original sixty-five Germans who set out for Mexico, only eleven made it home. Since the Kickapoo won their unnecessary encounter, the author may be mixing two tales.

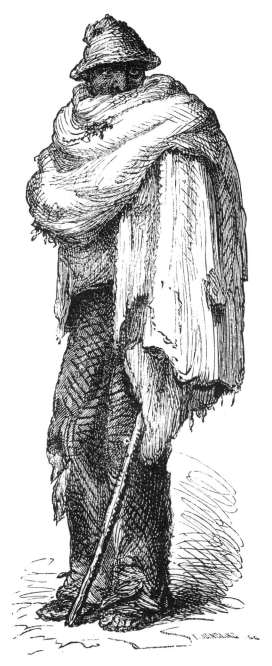

A Mexican Beggar.

between the towns of San Antonio and Eagle Pass, — a region embracing 30,000 square miles. They were wont to dash into the ranches and stampede all the stock they could frighten, driving it before them to the Rio Grande, and, although well-armed pursuers might be close behind them as they crossed the fords, they would usually escape with their prey, knowing that in Mexico reclamation would be an impossibility.

They came, and still come from time to time, within a few miles of San Antonio, to gather up horses; and if they cannot succeed in escaping with the horses they invariably kill them. At the full of the moon the Indians will usually enter the vicinity of the ranches, on foot, carrying their lassos. They hide carefully until they have discovered where the stock is, and then the gathering up is a speedy matter. An attempt at pursuit is folly, as the pursuer can only travel in the day-time, when he can see the trail, and the only hope of peace seems to be the extermination of the Indians.* The citizens gather at San Antonio, and discuss measures of vengeance; but it is useless.

The Rio Grande valley has always been the paradise of stock-farming. Before the Spaniards had left the Texan country, the whole section between the Rio Grande and the Nueces was covered with stock. The Indians were in

"The citizens gather at San Antonio, and discuss measures of vengeance."

those days employed in herding cattle; imagine one of them engaged in such a gentle, pastoral occupation to-day! As soon as the influence of the missionaries began to wane, the Indians ceased herding, and returned to their old habits of murder and rapine.

The United States Commissioners to Texas are of opinion that not only have the Indians been aided and abetted by Mexicans in their stealing from the rancheros of Western Texas, but that Mexicans themselves are directly engaged in the stealing. So great has been the loss from these causes since the war, that the number of cattle now grazing west of San Antonio is between two-thirds and three-fourths less than in 1866.

But the stock-raisers, despite the many dangers and vexations which beset them, are a healthy, happy set. Their manners have a tinge of Spanish gravity and courtesy; they are sun-browned, stalwart men, unused to the atmosphere of cities, and in love with the freedom of the plains.

Their herds of thousands range at will over the unfenced lands, and only once yearly do the stout rancheros drive them up to be examined, branded, and separated. Ownership is determined by peculiar brands and ear-marks, records of which are kept in the offices of the county clerks, and published in the newspapers. There is a stock-raisers' association which has decided on rules for mutual protection and aid.

In 1872 there were 450,000 cattle driven overland from Western Texas to Kansas, through the Indian Territory, by Bluff Creek and Caldwell, up the famous "Chisholm trail." In 1871 as many as 700,000 were driven across. The general value of "Kansas beeves" is $12 to $13 gold; but after deducting all expenses, the average profit on the "drive" is not much more than a fair rate of interest on the money invested. The cattle interest is rather heavily taxed for transportation, and suffers in consequence.

But few cattle are transported by sea, the outlet for the trade by way of Indianola having never been very successful. The Morgan steamships carry perhaps 40,000 beeves yearly that way. The two great shipping points in 1872-73 were Wichita, on a branch of the Atchison,

Topeka and Santa Fe railroad, at the junction of the Arkansas and Little Arkansas rivers, and Ellsworth, on the Kansas Pacific railroad. The whole country, at the time of transit, is covered with vast herds, which begin to arrive in Kansas early in May and await buyers there. A stampede is something which baffles description; you must witness it. It is a tempest of horns and tails, a thunder of hoofs, a lightning of wild eyes; I can describe it no better.

Merely to see a man on foot is sometimes sufficient to set Texan cattle into a frenzy of fear, and a speedy stampede; for the great majority of them have never been approached save by men on horseback. The gathering up of stock is no light task, as a herd of 75,000 cattle will range over an area fifty miles wide by 100 miles long. Large stock-raisers are always increasing their stock by buying herds adjacent to their ranges. Many persons make fortunes by simply gathering up and branding the cattle which the rightful owners have neglected to brand; cattle found unbranded, and a year old, being known as "Mavericks."

The origin of this name is very funny.* Colonel Maverick, an old and wealthy citizen of San Antonio, once placed a small herd of cattle on an island in Matagorda Bay, and having too many other things to think of, soon forgot all about them. After a lapse of several years, some fishermen sent the Colonel word that his cattle had increased alarmingly, and that there was not grass enough on the island to maintain them. So he sent men to bring them off. There is probably nothing more sublimely awful in the whole history of cattle-raising than the story of those beasts, from the time they were driven from the island until they had scattered to the four corners of Western

---

*The author's version of the origin of the term "maverick" differs in detail from the accounts of J. Frank Dobie and other historians of the longhorn. However, the spirit of the tale remains the same. As for Samuel A. Maverick, he held a degree from Yale, left South Carolina because of opposition to John C. Calhoun's nullification stand (a sufficient reason in the eyes of this editor), and arrived in Texas in time to fight in the first Goliad campaign and get captured by the Mexicans for two months. A signer of the Texas Declaration of Independence, he was, like his descendant, Maury Maverick, a mayor of San Antonio. In the Mexican invasion of 1842 he was again captured and held for more than six months. While in prison he was elected to the Republic of Texas Seventh Congress, and returned home in time to serve in the Eighth Congress. Later he served in the state legislature intermittently until November 1862. He died on September 2, 1870.

Texas. Among these Matagordian cattle which had run wild for years were 800 noble, but ferocious bulls; and wherever they went they found a clear field. It was as if a menagerie of lions had broken loose in a village. Mr. Maverick never succeeded in keeping any of the herd together; they all ran madly whenever a man came in sight; and for many a day thereafter, whenever unbranded and unusually wild cattle were seen about the ranges, they were called "Mavericks." The bulls were long the terror of the land.

The estimated profits of cattle-raising are enormous. Some authenticated instances are worthy especial mention. One man in the vicinity of San Antonio began in 1856 with 150 head of cattle; he now has 60,000, and is considered worth $350,000; Another, who began by taking stock to attend to for one-third of the increase, is worth about the same sum. One ranch, that of Mr. Kennedy,* some distance west of Corpus Christi, has an inclosure of 150,000 acres, the fencing for which alone cost $100,000. Many a stock-raiser brands 15,000 head of calves yearly. The profits of horse-raising, making due allowance for losses by Indian raids and American and Mexican horse-thieves, are even greater. The owner of a large horse-ranch near Castroville told me that he had repeatedly endeavored to get up an issue with the Indians, who often attacked his ranch – hoping to get them indicted and then requisitioned in Mexico; but their tribal arrangements prevent that. The chief alone is responsible for the bad deeds of all his warriors, and any quantity of indictments would never bring him to justice. An attempt to operate under the treaty made by Corwin, in 1862 – by which the Government authorized district judges to demand the extradition of criminals, – was equally unsuccessful. The Mexican officers on the frontier recognize no law, no authority except their own.

*Mifflin Kenedy, who came to Texas an an experienced steamboat pilot and captain during the Mexican War, remained to form a historic ranching partnership with Richard King. When the two men dissolved their partnership, they had built or bought twenty-six steamboats for their river trade, which among other products handled tallow from their vast ranch holdings. Later Kenedy became a factor in Texas railroad building. He died in Corpus Christi on March 14, 1895.

Military Head-quarters — San Antonio.

The head-quarters of such troops of the regular army as are in the Department of Texas, is at San Antonio. A chain of defensive forts extends from Fort Sill in the Indian Territory — in that section occupied by the Kiowas, Arapahoes and Comanches, — south-west and south to the Rio Grande, and along the Mexican frontier. Forts Richardson, Griffin, Concho, McKavett, Clark, Duncan, McIntosh, Ringgold, and Brown, are the most important posts, and each is well garrisoned with several companies of infantry and cavalry. It is at Fort Clark that the gallant Colonel McKenzie* has long been stationed. The close proximity of the fort to the river has somewhat troubled the raiding Indians; but they generally manage to pass between the forts without being observed. Cavalry scouts are constantly engaged along the whole defensive line; but the men and horses are but poor matches for the Indians and their ponies. There is no telegraphic communication from fort to fort; therefore the officers at the various posts

*At 25 years of age Ranald Slidell Mackenzie, number one in his West Point class of 1862, became a brevet brigadier general in the Union Army. He held several commands in post-bellum Texas, but is most widely hailed for having cleared the Comanche barrier from Texas between August 1871 and November 1876. He died in New Brighton, New York, on January 19, 1889.

are never capable of concerted action. The line of forts extending from Concho to Fort Sill is intended to protect against incursions from the "Staked Plains" district, where the Indians still wander at their own sweet will over the grass-carpeted plains, which are seemingly boundless as the ocean. The grandeur, the rugged beauty of these mighty table-lands will for many years yet be enjoyed only by the Indian; he makes a good fight there.

South-west from Fort Concho runs a defensive line, dotted with Forts Stockton, Davis, Hultman,* and Bliss, the latter opposite El Paso, at the extreme western limit of Texas, and nearly seven hundred miles from San Antonio, at the entrance of the mountain passes of Chihuahua. Service in this department is no child's play; it is a rough and tumultuous school; and to see the general activity, one wonders that more is not actually accomplished.

*Fort Hudson perhaps? Hudson was established in Val Verde County near Devil's River on June 7, 1857 to protect the road from San Antonio to El Paso from hostile Indians. It was abandoned in April 1868.

Railroads alone can solve the question. As it is, the thirty-five hundred men in the department, whether officered by General Auger, the present department commander, or General Grant, cannot catch and punish the evil-minded Indians. The soldiers are rarely attacked; the alert and logical savage seeks a peaceful prey rather than a fight with men as well armed as himself. Never advertising his coming, as the soldiers too often do, he rarely meets them. He is all eyes and ears; the tiniest cloud of dust on the horizon announces to him the approach of some one; he notes the faintest tremor among the grasses, and knows what it signifies; he detects a little imprint on the turf, and can decide at once whether or not it is that of a soldier's foot, or a white man's horse.

When he mounts a hill, he looks about to see if there is anything stirring on the plain; and if there be, he hides until he knows what it is. It is easy to see that recruits and unpracticed frontiersmen cannot fight such people as these. Very few soldiers are harmed; it is mainly the innocent settlers, who have no idea of protecting themselves, who suffer. Since 1866 over 300 unoffending Texans have been killed by murderous Indians and Mexicans.

Great care is necessary in traversing the plains, even with an escort of soldiers. A gentleman, returning from Fort Clark, once strayed ahead of the main party and was found, with arrows sticking in him and minus his scalp, dead. The Indians even hovered around the Government commissioners, on their journey from Eagle Pass to Laredo. For efficiency's sake, the Texans should be allowed in some way to take the matter of subduing the Indians and protecting their frontier against the Mexicans into their own hands.

Wonderful land of limitless prairie, of beautiful rivers and strange foliage — land where there is room to breathe full breaths — land beyond which there seem no boundary lines — the railroad will yet subdue you! Then there will be no more mystery in your plains — your chaparral thickets — your groves of post oak and pecan — your cypress-bordered streams — your grand ranges — your sun-burnished stretches. Stage routes will be forgotten; the now rapidly decaying native Indian tribes will stray into some unexplored nook, never to sally forth again. The Rio Grande will no longer be a boundary, and the Sierra Madre's rocky gaps will echo back the sharp accents of the American tongue. All this in a few years unless the tokens fail!

Scene in a Gambling House — "Playing Keno" — Denison, Texas.

IX

DENISON — TEXAN CHARACTERISTICS.

S TANDING in the main street of Denison, Texas, the
new town near the southern border of the Indian
Territory, six hundred and twenty-one miles south-west of
St. Louis, it was hard to realize that only four months
before my visit its site was almost a wilderness, not a building of any kind having yet been erected there. For all
around us was Babel — a wild rush of business, a glory in
affairs, an unbounded delight in mere labor, by which I
was at once oppressed and appalled.

The slightest indication of progress was pointed out
as a gigantic foreshadowing of the future preeminence of
Denison. "There are from 2,500 to 3,000 people here
now," said one gentleman to us; "how's that for four
months? That'll make some of the incredulous folks take
their frame houses off from the rollers!" — an expression
intended to open up a startling prospect for the future of
Denison. But, indeed, all these enthusiastic pioneers of a
new civilization were justified in their seemingly wild
prophecies of greatness. Northern Texas, under the beneficent influences of railroad pioneering, is assuming a prom-
inence which had never been imagined for it until within
the last five years.

As soon as the Missouri, Kansas and Texas railway
had crossed the Red river, a stream of immigration, which
the most sanguine had not hoped for, set in. The North-
west seemed to move *en masse*. The tracts of fertile, black-
wax land, which literally needed but to be tickled with the
plough to smile a harvest, were rapidly taken up, and Denison sprang into existence as the chief town of the newly
developed region. It was organized four months before my

visit, and since that time the Denison Town Company had sold $90,000 worth of building lots. The town stands in a county absolutely free from debt, and is at the outlet of one of the most fertile farming regions of the world. Two railroads, coming to it from opposite points, and not costing it a cent, laid the foundation for its remarkable advance, an advance more like magic than like the normal growth of a pioneer settlement.

All the lumber for the houses and business establishments was brought hundreds of miles, there being none suitable in the vicinity; and the car-loads of material were changed into rough but commodious structures in a twinkling. It was exceedingly remarkable, also, that in a community one-half of which was undoubtedly made up of professional ruffians, "terminus" gamblers, and the off-scourings of society, and where there was not yet a regularly organized government, there was not more of terrorism.

Every third building in the place was a drinking saloon with gambling appurtenances, filled after nightfall with a depraved, adventurous crowd, whose profanity was appalling, whose aspect was hideous. Men drunk and sober danced to rude music in the poorly-lighted saloons, and did not lack female partners. In vulgar bestiality of language, in the pure delight of parading profanity and indecency, the ruffian there had no equal. The gambling houses were nightly frequented by hundreds. Robberies were, of course, of frequent occurrence in the gambling hells, and perhaps are so still; but in the primitive hotels, where the luckless passengers from the Missouri, Kansas and Texas railway awaited a transfer by stage to Sherman, and where they were packed three or four together in beds in a thinly-boarded room through whose cracks rain might fall and dust blow, they were as safe from robbery or outrage as in any first-class house. Rough men abounded, and would, without doubt, have knocked any one upon the head who should find himself alone, unarmed, and late at night, in their clutches. But the carrying of concealed weapons is so expressly forbidden by the laws of Texas, that cases of shooting rarely occurred, and there was no more danger to the life or limb of the traveler than may be met with on Broadway. I was too late to see the Denison

"Men drunk and sober danced to rude music."

where rascals had held supreme sway. Their *regime* vanished when the railroad crossed the Red river.

The business men of Denison are a stern, self-reliant, confident company. They have a thorough belief in Northern Texas; intend to tame its wildness, and make it one of the gardens of the world. The Kansas and Missouri and Illinois and Western New York character crops out everywhere in Denison, and is the chief reliance of the town.

The aboriginal Texan looks on, and admires the energy displayed, but he takes good care not to mix in the fray too much himself. There is something sublimely impudent, charmingly provoking, in the manner in which he disappears from work and the street when a cold "Norther" comes on; in the cool, defiant way in which he forces others to work for him, and the utter surprise he manifests when he is accused of droning. He is a child of the sun; he dislikes effort; it gives him no gratification to labor in the rough ways of a new town like Denison.

Yet this same man can leap to the level of a hero when his rights are assailed; can bathe a San Jacinto plain with his best blood; can stand at an Alamo's breastworks until covered with wounds, and can ride at the head of a brigade into the very gates of death without losing one iota of his magnificent equipoise.

But the old population of Northern Texas is rapidly assimilating with the new-comers, and there is no longer any vestige of the intolerance which made a Texan regard a stranger as an intruder. Neither is it safe in a new town like Denison to judge a man, as we are forced to do in large cities, by his outer garb and manners. The huge hulking fellow with one cheek distended with tobacco, and with his clothes all so disposed that they seem to have been thrown upon him, will answer you with all the courtesy and grace of a high-bred gentleman, and will show a consideration for your opinions and your remarks which you do not always receive from the *habitues* of a city. The roughness is exterior only, and he who contents himself with a passing glance will not penetrate to the sterling qualities which that exterior conceals.

The earnestness of the new town, the almost religious quality of its ambition, were amusing as well as inspiring. Every one talked in exaggerated phrase; land values were fictitious; the estimates of immigration were overdrawn; the "probabilities" were certainly elastic, but there was such hope! Many men who had only been in Texas a year or two had already become rich, enhancing, at the same time, the value of property in the localities in which they had settled. In the little boarded newspaper office there was the same dauntless ambition; in the saloon, again the same. "Sherman ain't nothin' to this yer," said one man to me; "we've got the riffle on her on saloons." He could not even allow a neighbor town a preeminence in vice. "General Sheridan's going to build a supply depot here, 'n' then you'll see!" was the final, annihilating rejoinder administered to a carping Shermanite in our hearing. All the inhabitants were determined to make a magnificent city out of this irregular group of one-story wooden buildings, confusedly located on the high rolling land four miles south of the Red river, and their zeal was both to them and to us "like new wine."

He would, indeed, be a brave man who should, at this writing, prophesy that the great new route to the Gulf will redeem the Indian Territory from its present isolation, and bring it into the Union first as on probation, and finally as a State. Nevertheless, the people of the south-west are firmly convinced that such will be the case, and, for various important reasons, the inhabitants of Northern Texas earnestly desire it. The existence of such an immense frontier, so near to the newly settled districts of Texas, enables rogues of all grades to commit many crimes with impunity, for, once over the border, a murderer or a horse-thief can hide in the hills or in some secluded valley until his pursuers are fatigued, and can then make his way out in another direction.

So frequent had this method of escape become, at the time of the founding of Denison, that the law-abiding citizens were enraged; and the famous deputy-sheriff, "Red Hall," a young man of great courage and unflinching "nerve," determined to attempt the capture of some of the desperadoes. Arming himself with a Winchester rifle, and with his belt garnished with navy revolvers, he kept watch on certain professional criminals. One day, soon after a horse-thief had been heard from in a brilliant dash of grand larceny, he repaired to the banks of the Red river, confident that the thief would attempt to flee.

In due time, the fugitive and two of his friends appeared at the river, all armed to the teeth, and while awaiting the ferry-boat, were visited by Hall, who drew a bead upon them, and ordered them to throw down their arms. They refused, and a deadly encounter was imminent; but he finally awed them into submission, threatening to have the thief's comrades arrested for carrying concealed weapons. They delivered up their revolvers and even their rifles, and fled, and the horse-thief, rather than risk a passage-at-arms with the redoubtable Hall, returned with him to Denison, after giving the valiant young constable some ugly wounds on the head with his fist. The passage of the river having thus been successfully disputed by the law, the rogues became somewhat more wary.

"Red Hall."

"Red Hall" seemed to bear a charmed life. He moved about tranquilly every day in a community where there were doubtless an hundred men who would have delighted to shed his blood; was often called to interfere in broils at all hours of the night; yet his life went on. He had been ambushed and shot at, and threatened times innumerable, yet had always exhibited a scorn for his enemies, which finally ended in forcing them to admire him. When he visited me on my arrival in Denison, he remarked, "I shall see you in Sherman Monday, as I have some prisoners to take to court there;" but Monday morning, as I was starting for Sherman, he informed me that when he awoke in the morning, he was surrounded by armed men; a pistol was held under his nose; and he was told that he was arrested at the instance of the United States Marshal, to whom some one had been retailing slanders concerning him. Even as he spoke he was vigilantly guarded by armed men. But in the afternoon he was free again – once more in authority, and awing the ruffians into a proper respect.

The tracks of the great railway connecting Northern Texas with the outer world had but just been completed to Denison when I visited the town, but the huge freight-houses were already filled with merchandise awaiting transportation to the interior. The Overland Transportation Company was closing its books, for the Texas Central railway line was expected in a few weeks to reach the Red river, and the great Gulf route would be complete.

Staging to Sherman, we passed immense wagon-trains of merchandise, creaking forward through the wax-like soil, which clung in such masses to the wheels that the teams stopped from time to time, discouraged. Gangs of stout fellows from Illinois and Missouri were marching along the highways, *en route* for the railroad lines which they were to aid in constructing; mule-teams, drawing loads of lumber, each team driven by a six-foot Texan with a patriarchal beard, passed us; wild-looking men mounted on horses or mules, with rifles slung over shoulders, and saddle-bags stuffed with game, cantered by.

Sometimes we met a discouraged company, painfully forcing its way back toward sunrise, the *paterfamilias* driving a span of sorry mules which dragged a weary wagon-load of grumbling and disheartened family. So, faring forward through forest and brake, over creeks and under hills, beside smiling fields and along mournful wastes, into primitive clearings and out of forsaken nooks, and crannies where civilization had only made the wilderness look worse, we reached Sherman, the forty-year-old shire town of Grayson county.

Glorious sunlight enlivened the town as we entered it, and intensest activity prevailed, the county court being in session. The town is built around a square, in the centre of which stands a low, unpainted wooden building, known as the Court-House. The "grand jury" was not far from the aforesaid building, as we drew up at the hotel opposite it, and was to outward appearance a collection of rough, sensible farmers, impressed with a full sense of their duty.

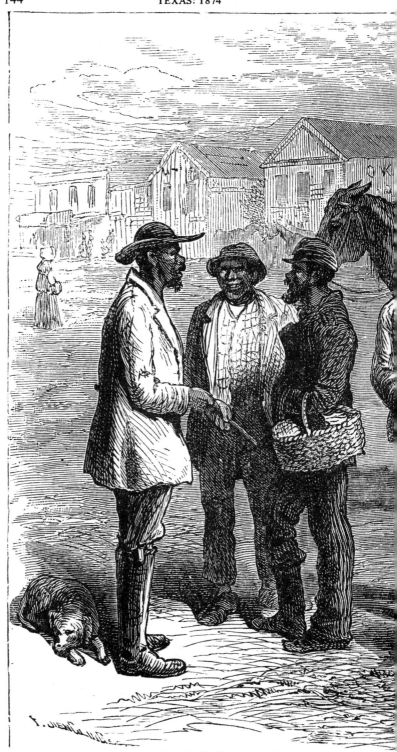

The Public Square in Sherman, Texas.

The horses on which half-a-hundred of the neighboring farmers had ridden in to attend to their marketing and upon the sessions of the court, were hitched at a common hitching frame not far from the court-house; and in the centre of the square a noisy auctioneer, whom the Texans were regarding with admiring eyes, was bawling out his wares. The plank sidewalks were crammed with tall youths, in patched homespun; with negroes, whose clothing was a splendid epitome of color; with spruce speculators — Northerners and Westerners — dressed in the latest styles; with dubious-looking characters, who shrank a little apart from the common gaze, as if afraid of the day-light; with swine, that trotted hither and yon; and with the hook-nosed and loud-voiced Israelites, who are found in every city and hamlet throughout the South.

Large numbers of people seemed diligently engaged in doing nothing whatever, or in frankly enjoying the delicious sunlight, which gave new glory and picturesqueness to everything upon which it rested. Now and then a soft breeze came gently from the uplands, and softened the effect of this generous sun. The excited gambler came out to bathe his livid face in zephyr and sunlight; the negro crawled to the sidewalk's edge, and with his feet in the mud, blinked like an owl in the fierce glare; the stage-drivers swore round but rather jocund oaths at the rearing and plunging mules drawing the coaches for Denison, McKinney, and other little towns; and the big negro who guarded the court-house door twirled the great key majestically, and looked ferocious.

Although it was midwinter, the day was as perfect as one in June at the North; but the languor which stole over us was purely Southern, as I imagined myself to be dreaming away the afternoon in lazy abandon and irresolute comfort, spiced only with the charm of studying new types of a common nationality. Toward evening there was absolute tranquility all over the place. Not even a loud word was spoken. The dusky figures who sat crouched in the porch of our hotel, mutely regarding the glories of the setting sun, seemed almost in the act of worship.

Denison was a yearling when I saw it for the second time, and the most wonderful changes had meanwhile taken place. The Texas Central railway line was completed. Northern and Southern Texas were connected, and Pullman cars were running through the untamed prairies. The gamblers and ruffians had fled. Denison had acquired a city charter; had a government, and the rabble had departed before law could reach them. A smart new hotel, near the railroad, was doing a driving business, hundreds of people thronging its dining-rooms.

Above Denison, at the river, another town had sprung up, a child of the Texas Central, and ambitiously named "Red River City." Newsboys called the daily paper about the streets of Denison; we heard of the opera-house; we saw the announcement of church services; and the notices of meetings for the discussion and advocacy of new railroad routes were numerous.

I confess to a certain feeling of disappointment in not having found more marked peculiarities in the people of Texas. There are, of course, phrases and bits of dialect which distinguish them from the inhabitants of other sections; but even the rude farmer in the back-country is not as singular as he has been represented. In extreme Southern and extreme Northern Texas, the visitor from the North or West sees but little variation from his own types in the cities; and yet in the remote districts he may find more ignorance and less idea of comfort than he would have thought possible in America.

There are a good many instances of rude and incult rich men; people who are of the old *regime,* and who, while owning thousands of cattle, sheep, and horses, live in log-houses, eat mean food, and have scarcely more than one suit of clothes in ten years. But these people are quietly disappearing before the newcomers. At first they are fierce against innovation, and indignant at frame houses, railroad stations and saloons; but finding that they must yield or retire, they acquiesce.

The general characteristics of an old style Texan farm were unthrift and untidiness; the land was never half tilled, because it produced enough to support life without being highly cultivated. When a fence fell into decay — if by some strange chance there was a fence — the rails or boards lay where they fell; people grew up like weeds, and choked each other's growth. Those who held slaves counted their wealth in "niggers," and sometimes boasted that they were worth a hundred thousand dollars, while living in meaner and more uncomfortable fashion than the poorest Irishman at the North.

The only amusement of the *paterfamilias* was a hunt, or a ride to the county seat in court time, where, in days when every one carried arms, there was usually some exciting event to disturb the monotony of existence — perhaps to disturb existence itself. There was no market, no railroad within hundreds of miles, no newspaper, no school, save perhaps some private institution miles from the farm or plantation, and no intellectual life or culture whatever.

The rich slave-owner was a kind of patriarchal savage, proud of his own dirt and ignorance. The heroic epoch of the struggle for independence being over, thousands of persons settled down to such life as this, and thought it vastly fine. What a magnificent awakening has come to them!

The mass of people in the interior still have a hearty scorn for anything good to eat. The bitter coffee, and the greasy pork, or "bacon," as it is always called, still adorns the tables of most farmers. A railroad president, inspecting a route in Northern Texas, stopped at a little house for dinner. The old lady of the homestead wishing to treat her guest with becoming dignity, inquired in the kindest manner, after having spread the usual food before him, "Won't ye have a little bacon fat to wallop your corn dodgers in now, won't ye?" This was the acme of hospitality in that region.

Now and then, in these days of immigration, a housewife will venture a timid "Reckon ye don't think much of our home-made fare, do ye?" when the visitor is a stranger; and, indeed, he shows upon his face his wonder that a well-to-do farmer's stout sons and pretty daughters are satisfied with pork and molasses and clammy biscuits, with no vegetables whatever.

The negro is responsible for the introduction of such oceans of grease into Texan cookery; it suited his taste, and the white people for whom he cooked mutely accepted it, just as they insensibly accepted certain peculiarities of his dialect, — notably "dat'ar" and "dis yer," and "furder" for further; mispronunciation which it makes one stare to hear good-looking white people use, as if they supposed it correct. The Texan has one phrase by which he may easily be recognized abroad: "I reckon *so,*" with the accent on the last word, is his common phrase of assent. In the country, when riding on horseback, and inquiring how far it is to a certain place, you will now and then be told that it is "two sights and a look," which you must understand if you can.

There is in Western Texas a more highly-colored, vivid, and dramatic manner of talk than in the rest of the State, doubtless the result of long contact with the Spaniard and Mexican. In parts of Northern Texas, too, among some classes, there is a profanity which exceeds anything I have ever encountered elsewhere. In Western Texas it is fantastic, and, so to speak, playful. I once traveled from Galveston to Houston in the same car with a horse-drover, who will serve as an example. This man was a splendid specimen of the Texan of the plains, robust and perfectly formed. There was a certain chivalrous grace and freedom about all his movements which wonderfully impressed one. His clean-cut face was framed in a dark, shapely beard and moustache, which seemed as if blown backward by the wind. He wore a broad hat with a silver cord around it, and I felt impelled to look for his sword, his doublet, and his spurs, and to fancy that he had just stepped out of some Mexican romance.

His conversation was upon horses, his clear voice ringing high above the noise of the car-wheels, as he laughingly recounted anecdotes of adventures on ranches in the West, nearly every third word being an oath. He caressingly cursed; he playfully damned; he cheerfully invoked all the evil spirits that be; he profaned the sacred name, dwelling on the syllables as if it were a pet transgression, and as if he feared that it would be too brief.

Even in bidding his friend good-by, he cursed as heartily as an English boatswain in a storm, but always with the same cheeriness, and wound up by walking off lightly, laughing and murmuring blasphemous assent to his friend's last proposition.

Some of the small towns in the interior are indeed trials to him who must long stay in them. My severest experience was in a Northern Texan "metropolis" — its name shall be spared — where the main hotel was a new board structure, without the suspicion of ceiling or lathing on the premises, and through whose roof one could see the stars. The front office was about the size of a New England wood-box; and when some twenty persons, variously impregnated with questionable liquids, had gathered therein, the effluvia became shocking.

In the long, creaking supper-room beyond, a dirty cloth was laid on a dirtier table, and pork, fried to a cinder and swimming in grease hot enough to scorch the palate, was placed before the guests. To this was presently added, by the hands of a tall, angular, red-haired woman, a yellow mass of dough supposed to be biscuit, a cup of black, bitter bean-juice named coffee, and as a crowning torture, a mustard-pot, with very watery mustard in it.

This, the regular sustenance, I suppose, of the unfortunate people of that town, was so unusually bad that I forthwith desired to be shown my room; and was ushered into a creaking loft, over a whiskey saloon wherein a mob of drunken railroad laborers were quarreling, and threatening, with the most outrageous profanity, to annihilate each other. To the music of these revels I attempted to lull my wearied body to repose; but did not succeed, and went to the four-in-the-morning train unrefreshed.

Even at the station my troubles were not at an end, for on venturing to expostulate with an *employe* for not checking my baggage, he profanely condemned me, adding that "It's mighty easy to get up a fight in Texas." Had I remained twenty-four hours longer in that town, it is my firm belief that I should have been accommodated with a complete and thorough exposition of all the eccentric features generally accredited to the society of the State.

The people of Texas suffered greatly from the war; thousands were ruined by it. Young and old together went to the fight, returning only to find ruin staring them in the face, and the poverty which was so bitter hangs by them still. The sudden fall from large fortune to day-labor, so general in Louisiana, smote Texas sternly. But never, on the whole, was a people more cheery. It is resolved to rebuild and to accept the advent of

"New men, new faces, other minds."

The beauty of the fair Southern land is but faintly shadowed in these pages. It is too intense to admit of transfer. But no visitor will ever forget the magic of the climate — never guilty of the extremes of heat or cold which we suffer in the North, and yet so varied that the most fastidious may suit themselves within home boundaries; one cannot forget the attractive wildness of the great western plains, nor the tropic luxuriance of the southern shore.

He cannot forget his pilgrimage to rock-strewn Mount Bonnell, Austin's guardian mountain; nor the Colorado running between its steep banks, with the wooded slopes beyond melting softly into the ethereal blue; nor the long, white roads, bordered by graceful live oaks; nor the bayous, along which the whip-poor-wills and chuck-will's-windows keep up lively chorus all night long.

Nor will one visitor forget how, just at dawn, he saw a troop of hundreds of Texan cattle fording a shallow stream, and leaving a track of molten silver behind them, as the sun smote the ripples made by their hurrying feet; nor how, by night, as the slowly-moving train stole across the country, millions of fire-flies flashed about the fields; how gaunt and weary emigrants gathered in groups around the camp fires; how, now and then, some weary figure, bent and ragged, stole up behind the train with pack upon its back, plodding its way toward the land of promise; how the darkies at the little stations where the iron horse stopped to refresh himself, sang quaint songs as they threw the wood into the tender; how mahogany-colored old women besieged him with platters, covered with antique "spring chicken" and problematic biscuits; how hale, stalwart old men with patriarchal beards and extraordinary appetites for tobacco, talked with him of the rising glory of Texas, impressing upon him that this is a mighty State, sir; fast rising to the lead, sir; has come out of the war

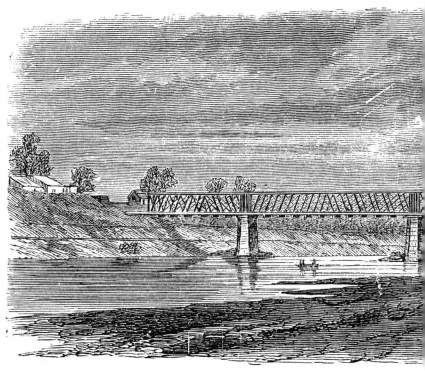

Bridge over the Red River – (Missouri, Kansas and Texas Railway).

gloriously, sir; and, sir, enough for all the world in her broad acres, sir; yes, sir.

Nor will he forget the motley throng of Mexican prisoners, straggling into the streets of Austin, charged with murder most foul, their great eyes glittering with demoniac hatred under the gray of their sombreros; nor the pretty maidens dismounting from their restive ponies at the "horse-blocks" in front of the shops, and trailing their long overskirts before the merchants' windows; nor the groups of negroes at the corners, chattering like parrakeets.

Nor the disguised army detective, slouching about the public places in the clothes of a western ranchero, prospecting for deserters; nor the gaunt teamsters from the borders of the San Marcos, the Guadalupe, or the San Antonio, with their half-melancholy, half-ferocious look; nor the erect military figure of "the governor," with his keen, handsome face and blond Prussian moustache.

Nor the typical land agent, with his bland smile and diffuse conversation about thousand-acre tracts and superb locations; nor the dusty and pallid travelers descending from the El Paso stage, their Winchester rifles in their hands, and their nerves strained with eight hundred miles of adventurous stage travel.

Nor can he forget how, one morning, on the banks of the beautiful Colorado, a ghastly cross-tree affronted the sky, while around a platform a great throng of white, and black, and brown men, American, and negro, and Mexican, gathered to see two men die. He will remember how the criminals came to the gallows and gazed round from the scaffold in search of some sympathetic desperado to help them; how, in his despair at finding none, one of them, in derision, broke into a shuffling dance, and after making a blackguard speech, fainted as the rope was placed about his guilty neck; how the crowd jeered at and mocked the two men until the scene was over, leaving the vacant gallows to stand as a perpetual warning.

Nor will he forget the moonlit evenings in the gardens of the southern coast, where the thick clumps of cedar joined their heavy perfume to that of the magnolia; where the rose and the myrtle vied in fragrance, and the dagger-tree spread its sharp leaves defiantly; where the snow-white of the jessamine peered from the darkness; where the China-tree showered its strange fruit on the turf; the fig put forth its tender shoots; the orange and the oleander, the verbenas and the pansies all looked coquettishly out of their midwinter beds at the Northern newcomer, seeming to smile at his wonder; where the grape trellises were covered with clinging vines; and where strange birds sang songs in consonance with the lapping of the waters on the Gulf shore, and with the intense hum of the unseen insect life, rising and falling like a magnificent harmony.

EPILOGUE

S O much of Author Edward King's personality comes
through in this book that the reader may feel he
knows something about the man after having read it.
Unfortunately, there appears to be no large body of
biographical material on King since, despite his obvious
reporting ability, he did not seem later to become one of
the immortals of American journalism. By any judgment,
however, he was successful and widely recognized in his
own time.

Edward King, according to his obituary notice in the
New York Times, was born in Middlefield, Massachusetts,
July 31, 1848. He got a liberal education, "and early manifested a decided talent for writing." At first he appears to
have written as much poetry as prose, which in those days
he probably "contributed" to various periodicals.

King seems to have been interested in affairs abroad,
judging from his subsequent career. Said the Times:

"Mr. King made a specialty of the physical character-
istics and present condition of the Southern States and of
French subjects, having resided for nearly twenty years in
Paris.

"While living there Mr. King acted as Paris correspondent for several American journals and accompanied
the Russian Army into the Balkans during the Russo-
Turkish war in that capacity. He was an intimate friend of
Hanry M. Stanley and Archibald Forbes."

Listed by the Times as King's works were such books as
"My Paris, or French Character Sketches" (Boston, 1868),

"Kentucky Love (1873), "The Great South" (Hartford, 1875), "Echoes from the Orient," poems (London, 1879), "French Political Leaders," (New York, 1882), "The Gentle Savage," (Boston, 1883), "Europe in Storm and Calm," (Springfield, 1885), "The Golden Spike," (Boston, 1886), and "A Venetian Lover," (London, 1887).

From these, we can judge that King was no beginner when he got his Scribner's assignment with Champney. He had, by 1873, two books already to his credit and appears to have traveled to Europe by that time. He must have been back in Europe within a few years after his southern U.S. travels since the Russo-Turkish War broke out in 1876, and he covered it as a correspondent.

King, reports his obituary, came back to the U.S. to live in 1888. The New York paper wrote in its March 29, 1896, edition: "Edward King, war correspondent and author of many books and poems, died Friday night at the house of his brother-in-law, John McGhie, at 151 Hewes Street, of Bright's Disease in his forty-eighth year. Mr. King had been ill for two weeks, but his condition was not thought to be very serious. He was reading an evening newspaper, when suddenly he became ill and died in a few minutes. . . the funeral will take place in Bridgeport tomorrow."

If King ever married, the obituary did not mention it.

About Champney, we know a good deal more. He lived longer and, at the time of his death, was considered a major figure in American art. The Times, in its May 2, 1903, obituary, allotted a substantial amount of space to the details of his career. It wrote that "James Wells Champney was born in Boston in July, 1843. At an early age he started as a wood engraver. In the Civil War he served with the Forty-fifth Massachusetts Volunteers. In 1866 he went to Paris where he studied under Edward Frere. After further studies at the academy in Antwerp, he returned to the United States and opened a studio in Boston.

"During the Carlist war he made many sketches in Spain. In 1882 he was elected an associate member of the National Academy. Among his earlier works, which gained for him a leading position in the art world were 'Which Is Umpire?' 'Sear Leaf,' 'Not So Ugly As He Looks,'

'Your Good Health,' 'Where The Two Paths Meet,' 'Song Without Words,' and many other favorites."

Times readers were reminded that three types of his "American girl" were then on exhibition at Knoedler's Art Gallery, 34 Fifth Ave. One gathers that Champney had a number of commissions in progress and that he was then at the height of his creative powers. His membership in a long list of prestigious societies and art groups, including the Metropolitan Museum of Art, testifies to his having "arrived" as a successful and seemingly prosperous artist.

Champney's demise was both bizarre and untimely. Reported the Times:

"James Wells Champney, the artist, was killed yesterday morning by falling down an elevator shaft at 5 Thirty-first Street. . . He was apparently in a hurry and disregarded the advice of James Kerr, the elevator boy, to wait for the next trip, as he was carrying a table on the top of the elevator for one of the new tenants.

"Mr. Champney said that the table would not bother him, and entered the car. The table, a large walnut piece of furniture, too large to be carried other than on top of the car, was held in position by an expressman. In some manner it slipped between the fourth and fifth floors. One of the legs struck the running balance weights, jamming and stopping the car. The wire ropes slackened and Mr. Champney found himself a prisoner. He waited for a minute and then opened the elevator door. Against the protests of the elevator boy, he attempted to swing himself to the floor below. He lost his hold on the car floor and fell down the shaft. . . the doctor said that he had not suffered, his injuries being such that death was practically instantaneous."

This happened only a few weeks before the artist and his wife were to have sailed to Russia for a lengthy visit. Mrs. Champney, the former Lizzie Williams of Ohio, was described as a litery figure in her own right, and the Times quoted her as saying "we were very happy together. He was one of the most beautiful characters in the world and was always lovable. His life was just like his work."

A photo of Champney at this time shows a dignified gentleman of austere mien with a flowing white handlebar moustache. He looked every inch the artist and his work got excellent reviews. The Century Magazine in its April, 1904, issue observed that "He was alive to what was best in art, and gave himself the means to study from the great masters of Europe, where he usually spent his summers, bringing yearly to his and our gain the beautiful copies he made of their works. . ."

Chapney was known particularly for his pastels. The Century's reviewer said that "it would be a good object-lesson if the best of his numerous copies could be held together and placed in a museum. This would also be a deserved tribute to one of the most prominent American exponents of the lovely, flowing, seductive pastel."

Champney's survivors besides his wife included a son, F. E. Champney, an architect of Washington, and a daughter, Mrs. John Humphrey, wife of a New York architect. The daughter, Marie, was a well-known painter of miniatures.

For those who may seek his surviving works in museums, Champney signed his earlier works "Champ" but later used his full name.

Champney's obituary also mentions how he had given a quick-drawing exhibition for the National Arts Club only a short time before his death. He may well have learned to sketch quickly from his travels through the south many years before. The reader of this book may have noted that King and Champney didn't waste any time any place. They worked hard and moved fast. They would have to have been encumbered with supplies of paper and the bundles of their finished work as they rode wagons, stage coaches and trains through our then-primitive state. They were members of a hardy breed of journalist for whom our rugged country was an all-consuming challenge to their skills. We hope they would be satisfied with this limited presentation of their efforts.   —RSG

INDEX